Life with Birds

Bronwyn Rennex

Bronwyn Rennex is a writer, artist and arts professional. She recently completed a Master of Arts (Research) in Creative Writing at the University of Sydney and awarded the Dr Colin Roderick Prize in Australian Literature, for the best thesis on a topic in Australian Literature. Her poems have been published in Cordite Poetry Review and her photographs have been exhibited widely and are held in private and public collections.

Until 2017, she was Co-Director of Stills Gallery in Sydney, where she worked with some of Australia's most celebrated artists. More recently she has worked as an arts worker/consultant in Arnhem Land.

Bronwyn Rennex

Life with Birds

a suburban lyric

UPSWELL

A catalogue record for this book is available from the National Library of Australia

NATIONAL
LIBRARY
OF AUSTRALIA

Front and back covers: Maree in our front yard, circa 1969, photographer unknown
Cover design by Chil3, Fremantle
Typeset in Foundry Origin by Lasertype

In loving memory of my father,
John Renfrew Rennex
1927–1980

and my mother,
Elsie Josephine Rennex
1924–1991

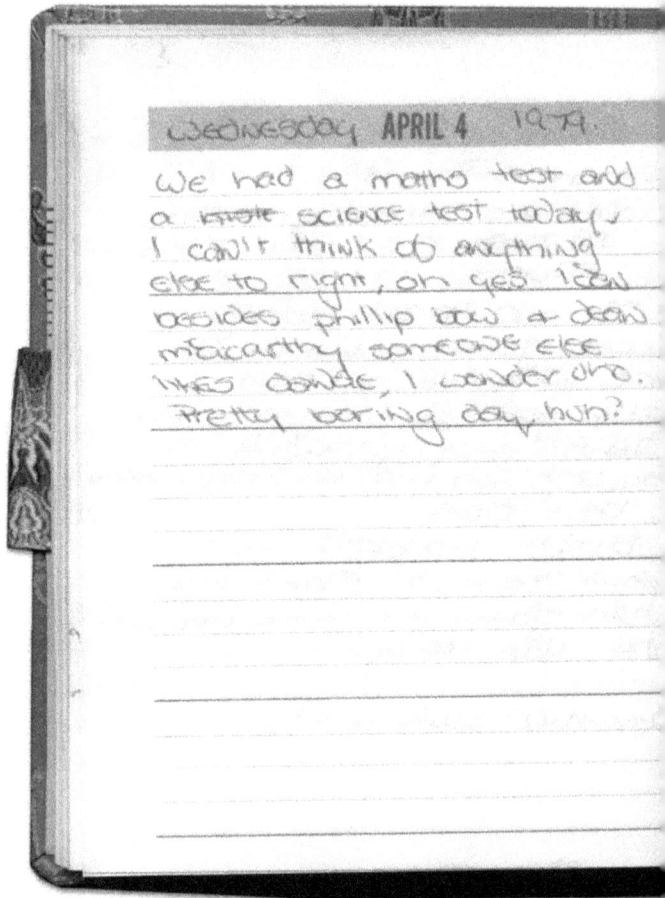

Wednesday April 4 1979

We had a maths test and a hist science test today.
I can't think of anything else to right, oh yes I can
besides phillip bow & dean mccarthy someone else
likes danae, I wonder who.
Pretty boring day, huh?

Thursday April 5 1979
NOTHING
HAPPENED

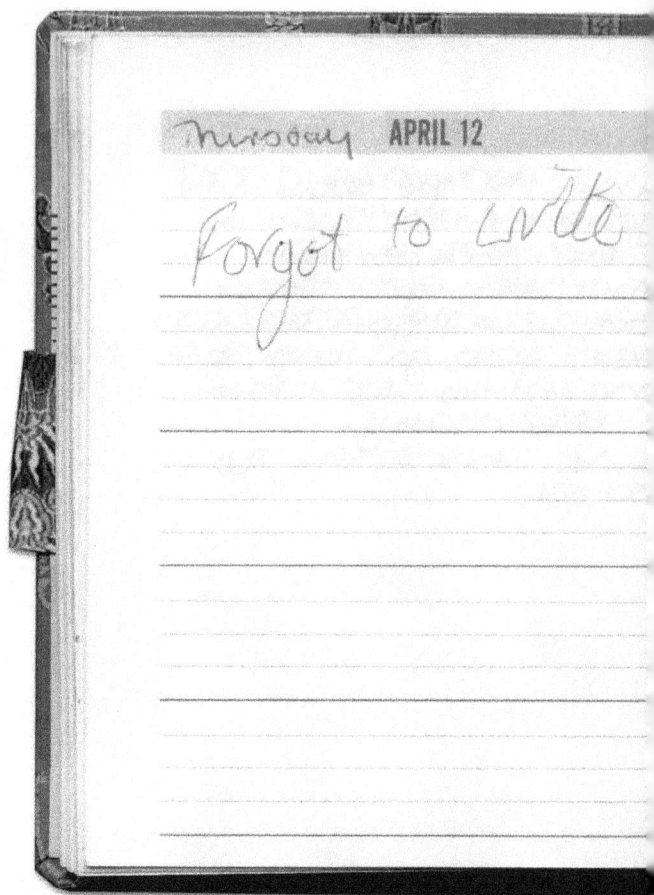

Thursday April 12

Forgot to write

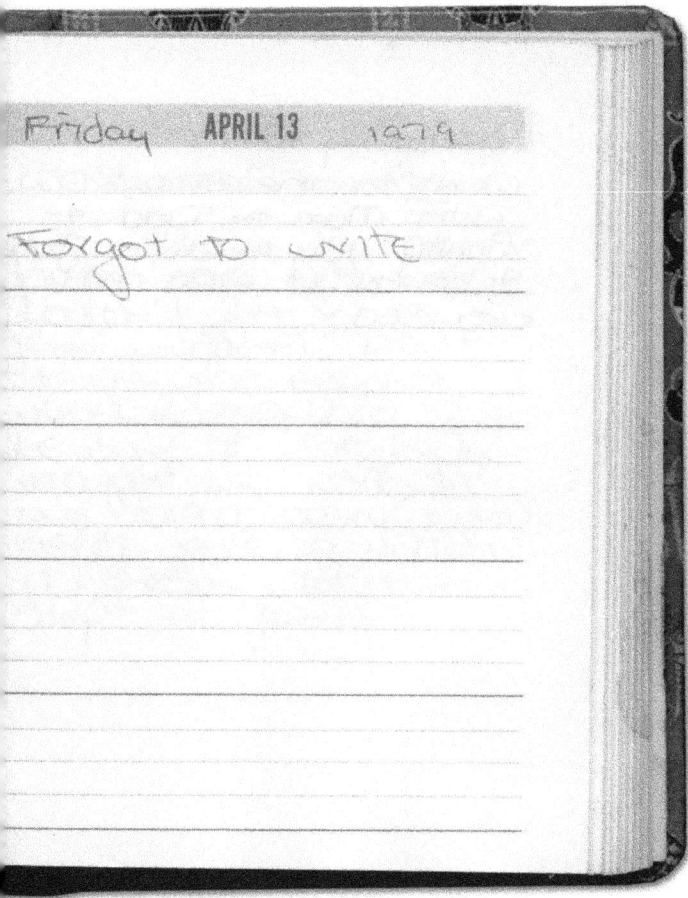

Friday APRIL 13 1979

Forgot to write

Friday April 13 1979

Forgot to write

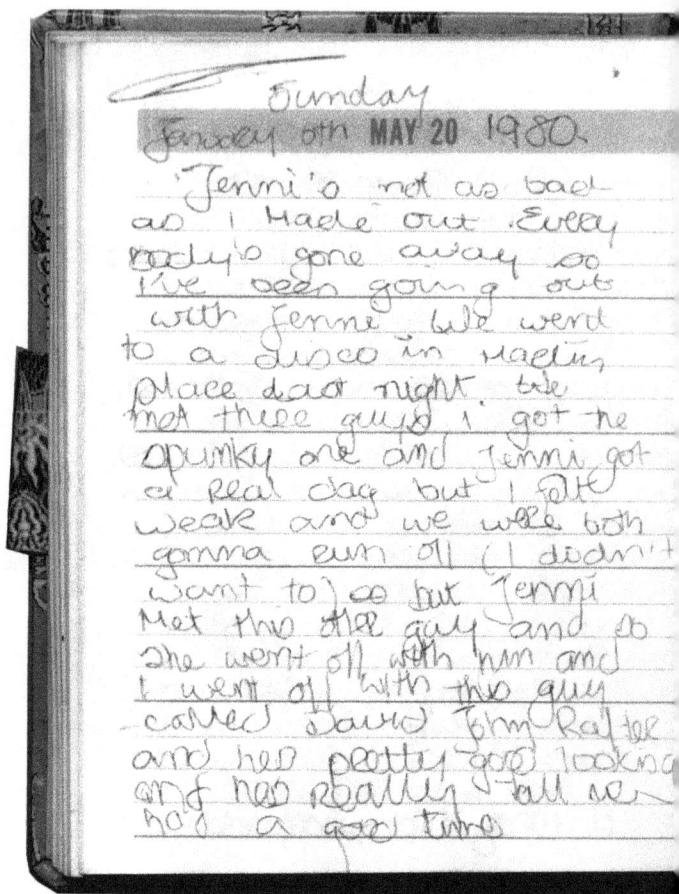

Sunday January 6th 1980

Jenni's not as bad as I made out. Every body's gone away so I've been going out with Jenni. We went to a disco in martin place last night. We met three guys. I got the spunky one and Jenni got a real dag but I felt weak and we were both gonna run off (I didn't want to go) but Jenni met this other guy and so she went off with him and I went off with this guy called David John Rafter and he's pretty good looking and he's really tall we had a good time.

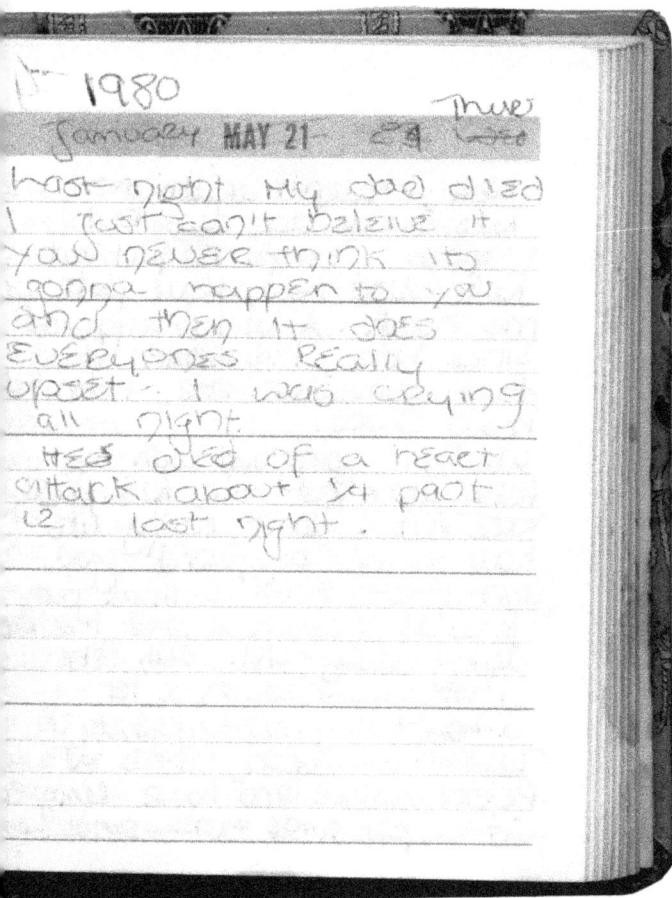

January 24 Thurs 1980

Last night my dad died. I just can't believe it.
You never think its gonna happen to you and then it does.
Everyones really upset. I was crying all night.
He died of a heart attack about ¼ past 12 last night.

The thing is,
it's not just me.
I'm one star,
in a galaxy.

On Wednesday 23 January 1980, when I was fifteen, I was woken by the sound of a dog howling. I lay in my bed listening to it for a long time. It went on, and on. Other dogs joined in. The whole neighbourhood seemed to be howling.

I got up to see if anyone else had noticed. My Uncle Gordon was there. He didn't live with us. What was he doing there?

He was walking down the hall towards me. Before he got to me,
I thought to myself,
'Don't let it be him that tells me.'

'I'm sorry, pet ...' he started.
Whatever else he said that night, he said it badly.
He said it wrong.

Turns out, it was my mum doing the howling.
Turns out, my dad had woken in the middle of the night with a pain in his arm or in his heart.
Something like that.

He didn't want to bother anyone.
Mum was worried, so she called our neighbour, Mr Mullens,
who drove him to hospital.

Dad died on the way.
He was fifty-two.

Earlier that night on TV: *Prisoner* – Episode #1.81

After Roz collapses, Kath puts her to bed but can't wake her next morning. Vera suspects she's been drugged; Greg takes blood samples and keeps her until they find out what the cause was. Kath has tossed the pen, and no one finds it; she pleads ignorance to Mrs Davidson. Bea tries to pump Kath for info, even trying to get Lizzie into the room with Kath and Roz ... While Leila fixes dinner, Geoff and Fletcher go to the pub... [1]

Birth marks

I was at an acupuncturist recently, getting treatment for the insomnia that had plagued me for months. Margaret, the acupuncturist, was a little bird of a woman, with long, grey hair that seemed to spring wild from her scalp. She was tiny and wise. She spoke slowly and softly. I lay on her treatment bed and she spent a long time feeling the pulse in one wrist and then the other.

'Your poor heart,' she said after a while, 'it's trying so hard, but it's not being supported.'

She started the treatment. Before inserting a needle, she'd lean towards the point of insertion and whisper, 'Breathe in.' I'd breathe in and she'd insert her needle, leave a moment for exhalation, then, 'Breathe in.' Another one. 'Breathe in.' Another. By the time she got down to my feet, I could hardly hear her.

She got to my left leg. I'd mentioned, when I arrived, that blood had started pooling in my feet and I'd been feeling a kind of woodiness starting at my ankles and moving upwards. It felt like my legs were trying to become tree trunks. She stopped and looked closely at my birthmarks.

'They must have had a hard time getting you out.'

'You mean they could have happened when I was born?' She nodded. You can hardly see them now, but when I was young my birthmarks were the colour of dark red wine, spilt claret. They ran from my knee to my ankle. I was always thinking about ways I could hide them. I wore long socks with tight elastic at the top. I avoided the pool. I dreaded summer and sandals. When people would say 'What happened to your leg?' or 'You've got something on your leg,' I'd say 'Oh them? They're just birthmarks.'

I guess I could have made up a more exotic backstory, but I just didn't want them to be a topic of conversation.

As I grew up, my legs grew too, of course, and the birthmarks faded. They came to look more like bruises than anything else – like temporary scuffs arisen from the rough and tumble of life. I'd always thought my birthmarks had been the result of a miscommunication of my DNA; that somehow, when it was time to make my legs, my genetic material got the colours wrong and put blush where there should have been beige.

On the drive home from seeing Margaret I realised there are actually five marks. One near my knee, in the middle of my shin and another four running in a diagonal line up from my ankle. Five fingerprints? My left leg is crooked too. Twisted outwards. What went on in that birthing room? Maybe I was dragged into the world, left leg first, kicking and crying. It wouldn't surprise me. Mum was forty when she had me – ancient in those days to be having a baby. She told me once, drunkenly, at a dinner for her birthday, that she didn't talk to Dad for two weeks after she found out she was pregnant with me. One of my aunties had told her to 'get rid of it' by drinking half a bottle of castor oil. Mum said she went home and had two tablespoons full and got the runs.

'Serves you right,' I said.

'Of course, I didn't really mean to. As soon as I saw you, I fell in love with you.'

'Which aunty was it?'

'I don't want to tell you.'

'Tell me. Who? Was it any of your sisters?'

She shook her head.

'Aunty Joyce?'

'No.'

'Aunty Elma?'

'No.'

'Aunty Mary?'

She looked at me and giggled. 'She didn't mean it. She didn't know you.'

'Bitch.'

The day I was born, 7 August 1964, the US Congress approved the Tonkin Gulf Resolution, which was the closest the US came to a declaration of war in Vietnam. The US claimed that their ships had been fired on by the North Vietnamese, in the Tonkin Gulf. Despite little evidence of an attack, the US Congress almost unanimously passed a resolution that gave President Lyndon Johnson power to escalate the conflict. The resolution was passed in the House 410–0. In the Senate the vote was 88–2. Democratic Senators Wayne Morse of Oregon and Ernest Gruening of Alaska cast the only nay votes. At the time, Senator Morse warned:

'I believe this resolution to be a historic mistake.'[2]

Before I turned one, my dad was sent to Vietnam.

He flew out of Australia on 1 June 1965, headed for Saigon.

Life Lessons #1 – counting to six in Japanese

One of the most beautiful things our family owned when I was a child was a green silk coat embroidered with bright red flowers. It was wrapped in plastic and wedged in the linen closet between flannelette sheets and beach towels. With its fabulous colours and extravagant sleeves, it was a peacock among pigeons. The only times it was liberated from the shelves was on cold winter nights when Mum used it as an extra blanket on my bed – and only when I asked for it. Coming from the suburb of North Ryde – a land of wood panelling, beige carpets and wall units filled with clown statues and crystal trinkets – the coat didn't just seem from another place, it was from another planet.

I thought the coat was a kimono and was related to my dad's time in Vietnam – even though I knew kimonos came from Japan.

My dad could count to six in Japanese and taught us how to as well. I could chant it to myself. *Itchy knee sand she go rocko.*

He had been in the army. He had been a projectionist. He had gone to Vietnam. He had a kimono. They were the facts as I knew them, facts I left untouched in my mind way longer than others might have. After all, they had a huge impact on my life. I didn't even know Dad until he returned from Vietnam – a different man, according to my mum. By the time he came back I was old enough to get on my hands and knees and bark at him like a dog, growling and tearing at the bottom of his trousers with my teeth, while he tried to hug Mum. I had no idea who he was. I don't remember much about being a baby, but I do recall tearing at those trouser legs. This odd-smelling stranger, entering my life, moving into my house, mauling my mum, hogging her attention, trying to cosy up to me.

A silent smoky battle

War service wasn't a topic of conversation in our house, particularly Dad's service. Whatever understanding I had of his wartime experience, I had pieced together – a photo here, an offhand comment there. I filled in a lot of gaps, and why would I fill them with anything but nice stories? I imagined Dad in a dark tent, just visible behind sparkling dust motes, projecting his light and sharing his stories with the tired troops. They probably all had nice warm kimonos on too, and some may have played guitar. My dad, the capable and kind guy he was, making sure everyone had a good time. Not much of a hero, nothing too traumatic either. Maybe he was a bit like Elvis Presley in *G.I. Blues* – he looked good in uniform and was fun to have around.

Though there wasn't wartime conversation around our house, there was army paraphernalia, including an old US army-issue khaki sleeping bag. It was mummy-shaped, tapered at each end, and when fully zipped left just a small round face hole, which made it perfect for dressing up as a worm. It was filled with feathers and smelt like men. There was a box of Kodak slides Dad took in Vietnam too (lost now – though a few were scanned before they disappeared). In that distinctive yellow box there were lots of pictures of bicycles, there were Vietnamese mothers with children, there was a haunted-looking monkey chained to a crate and a photo of the makeshift firing squad area outside of Dad's office – three poles sitting within a U-shaped configuration of sandbags, stacked to head height. That monkey was Dad's apparently. It always seemed quite human to me – the way it held the chains in its hands, the way it stared off into the middle distance, mute and trapped.

I poked around a lot as a kid. In Mum's wardrobe I found Dad's army tags stored in a black box along with the clip-on earrings she never wore. In the garage I found an old army medical kit with an empty morphine bottle in it. Dad spent a lot of time by himself in the garage, smoking, tinkering and listening to the *Goon Show* on the radio. He had any number of unfinished projects on the go, including a go-kart with an old Morris Minor car seat for the driver and a lawnmower engine and wheels. He stored his tools in drawers he'd made himself and labelled with nail polish (three daughters!).

My sister Maree told me recently that what I thought was a 'kimono' was actually a coat from Vietnam. It became another casualty of Mum's relentless need to edit. After Dad died, she got rid of it, burned it probably. She liked to burn things. She especially liked to burn things when the wind was blowing towards our neighbours at the back. The more smoke and the more washing on their Hills Hoist, the better. She thought the woman at the back did the same to her. In her mind, she was in the midst of a silent, smoky battle.

Dad's monkey (apparently)

Life Lessons #2 – Dad gives my 11-year-old sister Maree an impromptu lesson in self-defence while she sits on our back steps

1. *How to ram the heel of your palm up under the nose of an attacker – forcing their nose into their brain and killing them, if you do it correctly.*
2. *How to grab your attacker by the windpipe and squash it so they can't breathe.*
3. *How to brace your arms to provide maximum force when you gouge your attacker in their solar plexus with your elbow.*
4. *How to put your attacker in an arm lock to immobilise them.*
5. *How to dislocate your attacker's shoulder by grabbing their arm and pulling down on it really hard.*
6. *How to find and hold the pressure points in your attacker's neck to immobilise them.*
7. *How to break your attacker's arm by snapping it over your knee.*

Jungle warfare

I only really started to probe that childhood version of my dad when I was an adult with a child of my own. Both my parents were dead by then. There were two catalysts. The first was when my middle sister, Denise, who is into family stories, found out that Dad had served in Japan as part of the occupying forces. He was eighteen when he enlisted in Paddington on 7 June 1945 – two months before Hiroshima was bombed. He spent 795 days in Japan (news to us!) and he was a projectionist there – a member of the BCOF Cinema Unit.

The second catalyst came at my Aunty Ivy's and Uncle John's house one Christmas. We were lying around digesting and talking after lunch, when the conversation turned to my dad. Everyone loved my dad. Everyone still missed him. Even my mother's sisters would look at me with sad eyes and say, 'Your dad was such a wonderful man, so lovely … ' (No mention of my mother.) In response to a comment I made about Dad being a projectionist in the war, Uncle John said, 'Your dad wasn't a projectionist in Vietnam. He trained troops in jungle warfare.'

My dad? My gentle, quiet dad? The guy who never smacked us or even raised his voice at us? Why would Uncle John lie to me? Why would I only be finding out about that now?

Maree laughed, 'That explains why he taught me how to kill a man when I was about eleven.'

I can't remember how the conversation went after that. I think Uncle John got on to talking about his own exploits. When he worked in Defence he'd scared some heavies who'd come to Canberra looking for the Petrovs by saying he had a gun pointed at them under his desk and if they tried to enter the building, he'd blow them away. Of course, he had no gun, he told me. He then went on to tell me all about the best configurations of security grilles and then got back to my dad.

'He was a go-to guy in Vietnam. If you needed a problem sorted, he was your man.'

I was little. I was out with my dad at night.

It was dark, and I was scared.

'Dad,' I said, 'I'm scared.'

'What are you scared of?'

'The dark. There could be people out there in the dark. They might want to get me.'

'Don't worry,' he said. 'If you can't see them, they can't see you.'

Life with Battles #1

In the 1800s the area around North Ryde had a common called the Field of Mars. It was named after Mars, the God of War. Despite being originally intended for use by the community, the common became a popular place for squatting, hiding escaped convicts and making sly grog. In the mid-1800s the government broke it up and sold it off in smaller lots. The new roads in this reconfigured suburb were given battle names, in keeping with the martial tradition:

> Vimiera, Culloden, Agincourt, Crimea, Balaclava and a host of others from various periods of history, including the Hundred Years' War, the Peninsular War, the Crimean War, the Indian Mutiny, the Seven Years' War in Canada, various British campaigns in Africa, and miscellaneous other battles and British victories.[3]

Later, in the 1940s, North Ryde was home to a substantial army base, the 3rd Australian Ordnance Army Vehicle Park, which was essentially a vast car park for jeeps, tanks, transports, emergency motorcycles, generator sets, searchlights, and various military vehicles. After WWII, in the 1950s and 60s, the State Government bought and subdivided much of the land for Defence Service Homes and public housing.

Dad received a Defence (War) Service Home loan of $5500 in July 1959 to build our house. It was the only 'Defence' house on our street. There were other streets around North Ryde, though, that only had Defence Service Homes.

I've often wondered what happens when you build a suburb and populate it with returned servicemen and women. Would that place be any different to grow up in? Were the fathers in those suburbs any less likely to play joyfully with their kids, to participate in the wider world, to go to the footy, to take holidays on the coast?

Life with Battles #2

In our house, clothes were a battleground.

'Why don't you shave under your arms?' Mum would ask Denise when she wore singlets showing her luxuriant foliage. 'What will the neighbours think?'

'What do you want to dress like a man for?' she'd ask me when I took to wearing men's suits in my twenties. 'I wouldn't take out the garbage dressed like that.'

'Why don't you put on a nice dress and comb your hair?' she'd ask Maree when she was fashionably dressed in cheesecloth with an orange afro.

You had to admire her persistence. She maintained her fierce wish for us to fit her ideal of womanhood, even though she ended up with three reasonably smart, reasonably hairy feminists for daughters who all wanted to avoid being housewives for husbands.

'What do you want to go to university for?' she asked me after I enrolled in my first year. 'Why don't you go to secretarial college and learn how to type?'

The year of no talking

According to Mum's sister, our Aunty Ivy, Dad left the army because Maree didn't speak for a year. Ivy said the kids at school had teased Maree, telling her Dad would get killed before he could come home. Maree has no memory of it. None at all.

'Sometimes I think they misunderstood,' Maree says. 'I really didn't like my Year 1 teacher. It could be I didn't speak because I didn't want to speak to her.'

She does remember getting teased though. Kids would form a ring around her in the playground and chant, 'Sheep, Sheep, Sheep, Sheep,' grabbing handfuls of her curly orange hair. We work out how old we would have been. I was a baby and she was about seven.

'Maybe you were traumatised by me arriving?'

'No, I was traumatised by Denise. Apparently, I tried to smother her with a pillow. You, I just ignored … I do remember being chosen to do things more than the other kids. When I'd get chosen, I'd think, "Me? Again?" You'd think if I was being teased so badly that I didn't speak for a year, that I might have some memory of it, and I just don't. I just don't.'

Life with Birds #1

There were a lot of birds in North Ryde. Some lived in houses. The Starlings lived halfway up the road, on our side. They had no front fence and they parked their cars on the lawn. Mum thought their yard was a mess and often commented on their comings and goings. The Parrots lived at the top of the hill. The eldest of the Parrot kids was in Maree's year at school and was school captain. She was confident and competent but had an unfortunate resemblance to her namesake, her nose just a little too long, her tongue just a little too round.

The Woods had pigeons. Mr Wood, who I never heard speak, kept racing pigeons. He would let them out on Sunday afternoons. You would hear them before you saw them. A knot of twenty or so grey birds in the sky, circling around houses, flapping in unison. When he thought they'd had enough, Mr Wood would bang on a garbage tin lid and they'd all fly home.

On the uphill side of our house lived the Mullens. Mr and Mrs Mullens. Betty and Lloyd to the adults. They were both short and stout. Mrs Mullens was the sort of no-nonsense woman who wore aprons and didn't flinch when asked to cook tripe. My mum would pass a plastic bag of it over the back fence for Betty to cook for the men. Mum couldn't stand the smell of it or the spongy, brainy whiteness.

Mr Mullens was a bricklayer. His hairy forearms were covered with tattoos and he had a thick quiff of hair with a white stripe running through it, which he kept oiled and neat. Underneath his bushy eyebrows he had bright green eyes. If Mr Mullens had been younger, blonder and taller, with less prominent eyebrows, he might have resembled the Chesty Bonds man. Perhaps it was the fact they both wore singlets.

Mrs Mullens' parents, Mr and Mrs White, lived with them too. Mr White spent his life in a chair in front of the television. He was very deaf and old and even though his chair was just inside the back door, I didn't bother to acknowledge him, any more than I would have acknowledged the chair. Mrs White was Scottish and still had a strong accent. She'd say 'aye' instead of 'yes' and if you made the mistake of lingering long enough she'd tell you about her youth. 'When I was a wee lass ...' she'd start. Her memories of the past were in much sharper focus than the present. Some days she mistook me for one of my sisters, or my mum, or didn't even recognise me at all. After Mr White died, Mrs White spent more and more of her time on the Scottish heath of her youth.

Mr Mullens built himself an aviary that ran the length of his garage. He had all sorts of birds in there: Sulphur-crested Cockatoos, a Major Mitchell's Cockatoo, Cockatiels, Budgies, Lovebirds, Zebra Finches and Quails. When he was starting out, with just a few birds, he came over to our house one day and asked Denise if she had any books on birds.

'No, I don't think so,' she said.

'Oh, OK,' he said. 'Well, do you know if it's hard to join a library?'

Denise told him it was pretty easy, then he explained that he'd just cut up some apples to give to the birds he was keeping, for a bit of a change. The Rainbow Lorikeets went berserk when he put it in the cage. They attacked anything that came between them and the apples.

Turns out they don't eat seed like all the other birds, so that apple was probably the only food they'd had for days.

I watched Mr Mullens create a lot of enclosures within his aviary to keep some birds apart and others together. Quails and Budgies could co-exist, for instance, but a Lovebird would rip the legs off a Zebra Finch if it got half a chance. Budgies and Cockatoos would mate for life. They liked nothing better than to sit perched in pairs, preening each other in the sun. Once a partner died it was difficult to re-mate. Most of Mr Mullens' Cockatoos had a mate except the Major Mitchell's, who sat by himself in a section made of heavy gauge wire at the end of the aviary. A pale pink widower. The lurid colours of his crest rarely got an outing, but he was the noisiest bird of them all. His screeches and calls were the alarm clock of my youth. Each morning at sunrise or on nights of the full moon, he'd let everyone know he was alive and alone.

Life with Birds #2 – things I learned

Sharon Robertson lived across the road with her parents, Dan and Bonny, and her younger brother and sister, Warwick and Sandra. Sharon caught the aviary bug too – on a more modest scale than Mr Mullens.

At Sharon's house I learned:

- a bit about religion (they were Catholic)

- at Mass they put bread in your mouth

- some families shout

- how to clean a (their) swimming pool

- how to talk my way into a swim

- poo floats in pool water (well, Sandra's specifically)

- girl Budgies (hens) have brown above their beaks and boys (the cock birds) have blue

- it's good to have Quails in with Budgies

- Quails are bottom feeders, they eat all the spilled seed off the aviary floor and keep vermin away

- Quail cock birds are always horny in breeding season and you need to keep two Quail hens per cock, as one on its own would suffer.

I also:

- saw my first penis (Warwick's, in the bath)

- held bald baby birds, just hatched

- played doctors and nurses with Sharon.

Life with Birds #3

Our Budgie was ours by default. Mum was totally against all pets. She hated cats, even though they seemed drawn to her. She liked dogs but thought it was cruel to leave them alone all day, so they were out. Fish and birds weren't really worth the effort in her mind. The only reason we had a Budgie was because Denise found one sitting in the middle of Epping Highway on the way home from school. It was on the patch of concrete and grass between the three lanes heading towards town and the three heading north to the hills. She picked it up in her school jumper and carried it home. We called it Jellybean (2) and borrowed a cage off Mr Mullens to keep it in. There had been a Jellybean (1) for a brief spell, until Maree decided that it needed a bit of exercise and let it out of its cage to fly around. Jellybean (2) didn't like people putting their hand in the cage to change the water or food and would attack any intruder. I took to wearing a pink washing-up glove when it was my turn to do it.

Jellybean (2) only lived with us for a few months. One day, when I was home sick from school, I saw him sitting on the bottom of his cage. He was fluffed-up and breathing fast. I changed his water. I took his seed out and blew at all the empty husks to remove them, like I'd been shown. I topped it up again (food usually worked to cheer me up). He stayed sitting there, not moving. I called Mum at work.

'Mum, Jellybean (2) looks sick.'

'Oh, really, what is he doing?'

'He's just sitting on the bottom of his cage all puffed-up. Wait, I'll go have another look at him.'

When I got back to his cage, he was dead, a small green ball of feathers on the floor, lying in his own shit. I ran back to the phone.

'Mum, he's dead!' I started bawling. I'd never seen anything dead before.

'Do you want me to come home?'

'Yes,' I nodded, 'yes please.'

She came home, wrapped Jellybean (2) in old newspaper and put him in the bin. We ate the cheese and lettuce sandwiches she'd brought from work, watched the *Mike Walsh at Midday* show together and I felt a bit better.

Under fire

My friend Bea has been telling me about her dad. He has throat cancer. He is having radiotherapy. He catches the bus there. He doesn't have a job right now. This is the fourth time he's had cancer. Four different places in his body. He's trying to get an ex-serviceman's pension. She's helping him apply for it. He has to provide the Department of Veterans' Affairs with a history of his medical treatment, including from his time in Vietnam.

'As if you are going to remember the name of the doctor who treated you when you were on a battlefield,' she says. 'And the thing is, the government has the records. We have to get them off one department to give them back to another.'

Regretful sales

Regretful sale!!! *Unfortunately, I have up for sale my 2 year old beautiful tame male sulphur crested cockatoo. I have had him since he was 8 weeks old and have done all the taming and hand rearing. He does not bite at all. He talks, dances, goes outside and comes for drives and walks with me. He is so tame that I let him play with my 11 month old daughter. Unfortunately I have started a job that requires me to work 12 hour days and it has led me to have no time for him. He does come with a large aviary as well included in the price. For more information please call me.*

3 pcs galah cockatoo *swap to electric or acoustic guitar or any item or gadget that i may be interested to.*

Super friendly galah cockatoo
Super friendly galah cockatoo bird nearly 3 years old, talking always want to sit in the shoulder and asking for kisses, don't wat to leave but not enough time to ... $500

Male cockatoo, hand tame.
15 year old male cockatoo for sale, is hand tamed but only likes men, I am female so it doesn't work too well for me! Regretful sale, please message me if... $200

[Source: gumtree.com.au]

Mum's calls

Like a bird, Mum had some calls she made often:

1. Do (this or that) like a good girl.
2. If you can't say anything nice, don't say anything at all.
3. Only boring people get bored.
4. What do you want to do that for?

There were other suburban calls she only made once:

1. When she moved to the city from the country, Mum brought her yodelling habit with her, happily yodelling away in her bedroom until her new neighbours asked her to stop and she never yodelled again.
2. The first time she caught a double-decker bus into town, Mum sat upstairs. When the bus turned the first corner, she yelled as loud as she could, 'Grab your children, the bus is going to fall over.'

Stressed-out songbirds

In *The Wonder of Birds: What They Tell Us About Ourselves, the World, and a Better Future*, the author Jim Robbins rhapsodises about songbirds. He describes how, 'in most species the songs come prewired; in just a few – parrots, hummingbirds, and songbirds – their vocalisations are learned.'[4] If you raise one of those baby birds away from its parents, it grows up sounding nothing like the rest of the species. Robbins also writes about stress affecting the ability of Zebra Finches to learn their signature song. The more stressed they are, the less complex their songs become.

When Denise studied audiology, she developed a theory to explain the silences in our family. Mum had grown up in the country, one of six kids. Her mother was deaf and would often turn her hearing aid off for some peace and quiet. Perhaps, Denise speculated, Mum got used to not speaking or not being heard. Mum's father devised his own ways to escape the family cacophony. He'd either go to the pub to sit in the seat permanently reserved for him, or he'd say he had to go outside and count planes (they lived in the bush, nowhere near an airport). He'd stand by the fence in their paddock whistling to himself and tapping his leg, while imaginary planes flew overhead.

When Dad came back from Vietnam, he didn't speak about his time there. Not to us anyway. Faced with three young daughters and a wife, he retreated to work, or to the RSL or to the garage to tinker with one car or another. Apparently, he was pretty chatty outside the house and liked nothing better than a beer and a banter and a bit of a laugh. Who knows what happened to him when he got home. Mum once told Maree that Dad had never wanted children. Maybe Dad's primary relationship was with Mum and he wasn't that interested in us. Maybe that's why conversation in our house was mostly transactional.

It *was* hard to find common ground with him. We bonded over smokes and lollies. He smoked Rothmans Plain. I used to buy them for him at the corner shop. He'd give me five extra cents to buy lollies. I'd usually buy a few egg-yellow caramel buds, melt them in my palm then lick them up, and chewy caramel cobbers that got stuck in my teeth, clogging my mouth.

Rissoles and Budgies

My best friend in high school was Janet Clark. She was my soulmate. We did everything together. I loved her then and still miss her now. She died of some sort of brain infection in her early twenties as a result of a long-term addiction to heroin. She went downhill after her mum died of cancer, her dad turned to drink, her eldest brother to dope and her youngest to house-cleaning. He'd use brand names as verbs, which we found hilarious. 'I'm going to *Shake N' Vac* the carpet,' he'd tell her, 'then I'll *Spray N' Wipe* the surfaces.'

We discovered drugs together, and music and boys and sex. We'd make fun of everything, including ourselves. We laughed about the banalities of our lives. Once my mum got us holiday jobs on the production line at Schwarzkopf where she worked bottling hair products. It went fine until the day we started giggling about something and couldn't keep up with the machines. The bottles just kept powering towards us, which seemed hilarious and only made us laugh harder. We caused an avalanche of bottles and lids and conditioner that sent production into disarray and ended our Schwarzkopf careers.

Janet and I used to laugh at our dads when they went to the RSL. We called it the Rissole. We thought they looked like Budgies lined up to drink at a pond. Big chests and bellies, scrawny legs, brightly coloured shirts and shorts, long socks and laced shoes. They'd gather together and squawk in a language we didn't understand.

First visit to the Australian War Memorial

I decided to visit the Australian War Memorial to see what I could find out about Dad. It was school holidays when I went, and even though I had left Sydney at dawn to drive to Canberra, the car park at the War Memorial was already full when I got there. My bag was searched at the entrance and I tapped my credit card to pay the $5 'donation' for entry. I headed straight downstairs, 'through Afghanistan and behind the big painting' (as directed by the attendant) to the research centre.

It wasn't my first visit to the Memorial. A few years earlier I'd caught the bus down to Canberra and hired a pushbike to get around. I was staying at University House at the Australian National University. As I rode up to the entrance, past people sitting in groups enjoying the sun, I felt a whoosh of air and something black and white fluttering beside my face. It was a Magpie. For some reason, it wasn't interested in the other people sitting around chatting, just me on the bike. It turned and swooped, then swooped again. And again. I was already precarious, with a heavy backpack on and a bag over my shoulder, but I tried holding the handlebars with one hand and waving the other arm around yelling, 'Get out of here – fuck off'. The bird kept swooping so I had to drop the bike in front of the bemused onlookers and run inside to escape. For the rest of my stay there, the same bird (I assume it was anyway) would swoop me each time I entered or left the building, leaving everyone else alone. I developed a bit of a Magpie phobia during that visit and even now, when I walk past one, I cringe a little.

This visit, I didn't really know what I was looking for. Evidence of my dad being in Vietnam, I guess. Anything about his time there and what it was like for him. As you enter the research area there's a cluster of computers and tables to the right, staffed by volunteers who help people research family members who have served (mostly in WWI it seemed.) One of the volunteers asked me if I needed help and I told him I was hoping to find out something about my dad's experiences in Vietnam.

'Oh, that's too recent for us,' the man said.

To Think About

1. *This is often what happens:*
   War makes us afraid.
   We do not talk about it but hold fear in.
   Those who are sensitive to us get our feelings.
   They know that something is wrong, but they
   do not know what.

   > This shuts them out.
   > It makes them feel isolated, alone, un-
   > trusted.

   > It makes them feel a loss in status and
   > belongingness. It makes them resentful
   > toward us for shutting them out.

2. *This is what we can do instead:*
   Set ourselves straight as to what it is that
   we fear.

   Talk about it. Share it. Let those who are close
   to us in on what is wrong.

   > This sets them straight. They find it
   > easier to take the actuality of what we
   > tell them than to stand the possibilities
   > that lie in that which we do not tell them.

3. *We need to realize that trust and confidence and love
   are far more reassuring to children than long explana-
   tions and denials of danger.*

4. *We need to encourage children to talk out and play
   out their fears.*

   GETTING FEAR OFF THEIR CHESTS
   CAN HELP OUR CHILDREN LIVE
   MORE COURAGEOUSLY
   THROUGH THE WAR.

The list

Dad's army tags were kept in a square, satin-lined jewellery box, next to a pair of Mum's old fake-pearl clip-on earrings, a belt buckle engraved with bamboo and an army badge. There were two tags attached to a thick khaki string. They had the same engravings on them.

26425 METH J.R. Rennex on the front.
A2 POS on the back.

Idle and curious one day, I googled his name and army number. Not a lot came up, but I did find a list. An Excel spreadsheet named 20130630 Mortality Without Units (shared).[5]

Along the top of the pages were the headings *Name, Rank, Serial Number, Date of Birth, Date of Death, Age at Death* and *Cause of Death*. At the bottom there were tabs for *Army, Navy* and *Airforce*.

I started reading the *Cause of Death* list in the *Army* tab:
Liver Failure
Cancer Related Death
Motor Vehicle Accident
Cancer Related Death
Suicide
Motor Vehicle Accident
Killed in Aircraft Accident Nth Queensland
Cancer Related Death
Heart Attack
Suicide
Suddenly/peacefully at his home

Cancer Related Death

Leukemia

Stomach Cancer

Pancreatic Cancer

Suicide

Cirrhosis

Motor Vehicle Accident

Heart Attack

Heart Attack

Heart Attack

Cancer

Suddenly

Cancer Related Death

Brain Tumour

Heart Attack

MVA

Suddenly on Visit to Vietnam

Suddenly Cancer Related Death

Drowned

Emphysema

Liver Failure

It went on and on.

I found Dad's name – number 4813 on the *Army* list.

Born 10 Apr 27

Died 24 Jan 80

Age at Death – 52

Cause of Death – *Heart Attack*

When I sorted the *Age at Death* list from youngest to oldest, the *Cause* list started with a lot more *Killed in Actions (KIAs)* and *Motor Vehicle Accidents (MVAs)*. As I scrolled down, there were still lots of *MVAs* but also more *Suicides*. Down further and the cancer-related deaths started popping up, and then heart attacks. Right at the end, people started dying after long illnesses or going peacefully. Then last of all there were blanks, for people who were still going or unknown, I guess.

Cause of Death could be *cancer* or *cancer-related death*. Other times it was *After a short battle with cancer* or *After a courageous fight with cancer* or sometimes a specific cancer like *Stomach Cancer* or *Pancreatic Cancer*.

It could be *Suddenly*, or *Suddenly on a Visit to Vietnam* or *Suddenly Cancer Related Death*.

Suicide was mostly just *Suicide* but there was also *Suicide (rifle)*.

Heart Attack, in the same way, was mostly *Heart Attack* but could also be *Heart Attack/in WA Cyclone* or *Massive Heart Attack*.

There was also:
Died in the Netherlands
Stung by Bee
Whilst Playing Tennis
After Profound Suffering
Killed by a Water Buffalo in the Philippines
Succumbed to His Wounds from Vietnam

Strange thing about facts – it's like they are made of water. In stories, amid adverbs and action, they can flow over and around things. In spreadsheets they are like ice.

Cold. Hard. Solid.

When I found that list and saw how many other heart attacks there were, I thought about all the other daughters and sons who had woken to the same news that I had. Who'd had to go to school and have friends not know what to say to them and avoid them rather than get awkward. That's a lonely place. I don't blame people. We're not taught how to deal with death and dying. I didn't go to my dad's funeral. Mum didn't want me to. She didn't want Denise to go either. While other people were seeing my dad off, we were sitting at home watching TV.

Pink and peaceful

I ask Maree what she remembers about the night Dad died. She says she'd been out and when she pulled up outside the house, the front light was on. She remembers thinking, 'That's odd.'

'Mum was a mess,' she says, 'so I had to go up to Ryde hospital and do the formal identification.' When she got there, Dad's body (or is it still just Dad?) was laid out on a steel table. 'The only other thing I remember,' she says, 'is that he looked peaceful and he was quite pink. I was glad he looked peaceful.'

The next day she had to ring the place that he'd booked to go on holidays with Mum. He'd only booked it the day before. Mum asked her to call them, cancel it and tell them what had happened.

A woman of letters

Mum left school at fourteen. Her family was poor, and she needed to earn money. She went to work in a convent scrubbing floors. That must have been where she honed her lifelong resentment of housework. Not that our house wasn't neat – it was. Anything more than the basics though, scrubbing a floor for instance, my mother would do in a funk that was almost tangible.

She was smart and one of the most lateral thinkers I know (once, her friend couldn't work out how many balls of wool she needed to knit a copy of a jumper, so Mum weighed the jumper and divided it by the weight of the balls of wool her friend wanted to use), but Mum never had any more formal education after fourteen and spent her working life on production lines: at publishers packing books, at pharmaceutical companies packing drugs and finally at Schwarzkopf in North Ryde, packing hair products. She screwed lids on bottles of shampoo and conditioner and eventually became the supervisor of other women screwing lids on bottles.

Mum told me once that her doctor had prescribed her sedatives after Dad died. It was only because she was working on an assembly line in a pharmaceutical company that she knew what she had been given. She flushed them all down the toilet.

She had a way with disposal.

I'm not sure whether it was the inclination or the means she lacked to further her education. Perhaps it was a bit of both – after all, this was the woman who urged me to go to secretarial college rather than university.

I've been thinking about Mum's education a lot lately, wondering how she felt about the letter she had to write to the Department of Veterans' Affairs to claim a War Widow's pension. I never saw the letter and had no idea what was in it, except that I'm sure she would have said my dad came back a *changed man*. He didn't smoke before he left and when he got back, he did. He didn't drink either. And then he did. He talked a lot and then he didn't.

I was aware Mum worked on that letter for quite a while, with the help of a man from Legacy. I thought the man had too many opinions about what Mum and I should do, so I wasn't keen on him – even though (apparently) he offered help, not just opinions.

Mum didn't write much at all – it wasn't her means of expression. Cooking wasn't her medium either. Or sewing. But she could play a tune on the piano without music and she could coax the most beautiful flowers out of the azaleas and gardenias in our front garden. She did write letters to my father when he was away on army duties just after they had married, and before any of us kids came along. They were love letters. He kept them all. There might have been lots of them. I'll never know. She tried to burn them all after he died, but Denise salvaged one or two.

BURWOOD
10·30 AM
1 DEC
1953
N.S.W. AUST.

SEND MO
BY POSTAL NO
OR MONEY OR

2/6425
T/Sgt. J. R. Rennex
R.A.A.S.C. School
Puckapunyal.
Vic.

18 Hillcrest Ave.
Enfield
Man.

My own Darling Husband.

how are you my
sweetheart, not long now is it, five more
nights. Golly I can't believe you'll be home
at the week-end. I bet you're glad all
the exams are over, I'll be anxious to
know how you got on.

Another letter to-night. Gee my darling
Husband is doing fine. I wont write
any-more letters after this one darling
as it will be Tuesday when I post it
and probably Thursday when you receive
it and I don't know when you will be
leaving. so don't think I have suddenly
forgotten you or anything like that
darling. even though I wont be writing
I'll be thinking of you all the time.

Midge had a letter from Mum
to-day and she said the Stans would
be in Sydney to-day. Mr. Stan is in a

18 Hillcrest Ave
Enfield
Mon

My own Darling Husband,

how are you my sweetheart, not long now is it, five more nights. Golly I can't believe you'll be home at the week-end. I bet you're glad all the exams are over, I'll be anxious to know how you got on.

Another letter to-night. Gee my darling Husband is doing fine. I won't write any more letters after this one darling as it will be Tuesday when I post it and probably Thursday when you receive it and I don't know when you will be leaving, so don't think I have suddenly forgotten you or anything like that darling. Even though I won't be writing I'll be thinking of you all the time.

Midge had a letter from Mum today and she said the Stones would be in Sydney to-day. Mr Stone is in a bad way and he is losing a lot of blood. We haven't seen them yet. Mum will be down in the morning.

I hope you received the two pounds all right.

Gee it's been cold here today and looks a lot like rain to-night. I hope you don't find it cold travelling in summer uniform coming home. I guess your great coat will be handy.

Well my very own sweet precious darling Husband I guess this is the end of my Puckapunyal Correspondence. I've felt you haven't been quite so far away by writing every night, although I miss you more than I can tell, still darling it's nearly over. And Saturday can't come quick enough. So until then my sweetheart look after yourself and hurry home to a wife who adores and loves you so very much.

All my love darling
xxxxxxxxxxxxxxxxxxxxxxxxxxx your ever loving wife xxxxxElse xxx

My Darling Johnny

How are you sweetheart
Gee I couldn't believe my good fortune when I got a letter yesterday and another one to-day. Sure was good. A week to-day and we'll be together again. Wont it be wonderful. I get so excited I feel sick when I think about it. I enquired at Strathfield last night about whether the train stopped there or not and the chap I asked was very young and he looked up the time-table and it had Strathfield 10.39. He didn't seem to know much about it but according to the time-table I think it always stops there. If it doesn't I'll run after it all the way into town.

Last night Mary, Edna and Ericka came to my place for tea and then we met Gwen at Burwood and we went out to Jean Neilson's by taxi. Only cost us 2/- each we had quite a nice evening. Gee I don't know who can talk the most Nancy or Jean between the two of them the rest of us didn't have much to say. But still they're both funny. Nancy said to ask you are you still looking for a man for her.

Coming home I caught the train from Bankstown to Strathfield, then I caught a taxi. First in the taxi was a horrible old man then I got in with a young couple. Off we go and we were just about at Hill St and the old chap said Driver I hired you first and you needn't bother dropping anyone else off first you'll take me to my stop first and that was Lakemba, so the taxi driver could do nothing else but as the chap said because he was first in the taxi. So I had to go right to Lakemba and he dropped me off on the way back. Gee he was hostile with the old chap not to his face though. Wasn't he a miserable old cow.

Gordon just came in and asked me if I thought you would like to take over his Seasons Railway ticket as he is putting it in and getting a refund and I said you didn't know whether you would be getting a pass or not so it would be best for him to put it in. I don't know when he expects to paint his house he hopes to be going in the Navy in January.

I went into Grace Bros this morning and paid another instalment. I haven't done anything about the ring yet I'll wait until you come home darling.

Well my precious one I must bring this to a close for now it's Saturday and I'm just off to Rodd Point to see how Dale is she has been very sick and isn't allowed to leave the home so I must go and see what's wrong so darling cheerio for now. Look after yourself for me all my love sweetheart.

Xxxxxxxxx Your ever loving wife xxxxxxxxxxxxxxx Else xxxxxxx

I love my mum's writing. Amid the torrents of love and affection for my dad, there's the solid shoreline of the everyday – the time, the weather, transport options, health updates. I guess, for her, sticking to the facts made sense. Like someone who can't swim crossing an unfamiliar river and finding solid stones to rest their feet on along the way.

When it came to her making a claim for a War Widow's pension, what did she say? In the middle of her grief, how did she find the words to explain that, even though it was thirteen years after he had returned from Vietnam, her husband, her dear sweet darling husband had changed, and those changes had led to him having a heart attack at the age of fifty-two and dying on the way to hospital?

What if it was a love letter?

I was in a non-fiction writing workshop recently and the teacher was speaking about ethics. She had firm ideas about what was and wasn't ethical. What was and wasn't OK. She asked for questions from the participants and I raised my hand.

'What's your position on using a letter from someone, to someone else, not me, if both people are dead?'

'That depends,' she said.

'What if it was my parents? What if it was a love letter?'

'Well, I guess it would depend on how your siblings felt about it. Would they be OK with you making it public?'

'I'm sure they would … but what if the person who wrote the letter wouldn't … if they were alive?'

'Oh … that's a tough one,' she said, 'I don't know if I can answer that.'

What would Mum say if she knew I wanted to share her letter to Dad? After all, she destroyed most of the correspondence between them. How much of her story is mine to tell? I've thought about that question a lot since that workshop and … well … I'm fine with my decision. She'll never know. Dad will never know. My sisters know, and they don't mind. I spoke to Denise about it the other night. We laughed about me feeling a need to counter my possibly negative version of Mum with her own voice, one full of love for my dad, full of transport options and weather updates. Who better to speak for her than herself?

Shades of grey

Disappointment comes in many shades. Most of them are grey. There are thundercloud greys of rejection and resentment, the soft Pigeon grey of a missed opportunity, and then there is the shade of grey my mother told me about one day.

I had taken her to the Royal Easter Show. She was in the process of being treated for cancer. She'd already had a mastectomy, but the cancer had returned a year later in her spinal fluid. The doctors had to drill a hole in her skull, so they could put a little reservoir in there and pump the chemotherapy directly into it. As a result of the treatment, Mum's hair had fallen out and she'd started to wear a wig.

The wig closely resembled her earlier hairdo, so I don't think she minded too much, and maybe even found it kind of convenient. Mum's original hairdo was re-created every Friday afternoon by the hairdresser down the road. It involved a lot of curlers and hairspray, a few white wines and the occasional perm. The end result was a helmet of neat beige curls. Even when her hair started to grow back, straight and white, my mother continued to wear the wig.

At the Easter Show, I was trying to show her a good time. I had dressed up especially, but she didn't seem to have noticed. In the afternoon we sat down to rest on a bench in the Festihaus Beer Hall.

'Do you like my shirt, Mum?' I asked. It was a grey shirt with white polka dots, and I had on a matching grey hat. I thought it was all rather fetching.

She pointed at the grey of the shirt with her arthritic finger and said, tapping slowly on it, 'That's exactly the colour of your father's face when I went to see him after he died.'

(Great, I thought, I'm wearing a corpse-coloured shirt.)

'I didn't know you went to see him.'

'Yeah, I did,' she said, 'I wanted to. I went with Mrs Mullens and someone else. I can't remember who. That's why I hate the colour grey. I can't stand it.'

We finished our drinks and made our way to the Ferris wheel. Once we got to the top, there was a stiff breeze, and Mum had to hold on to her wig to stop it from blowing off. It was hard to be angry with her, even though I would have liked to. I sat opposite her in the cage, watching her giggle and clutch at her wig. It became a bit awry in the process, leaving her straight white undergrowth sticking out around the edges.

Hooray

I want to see if I can find Mum's application for a War Widow's pension, so I visit the closest Department of Veterans' Affairs (DVA) office to apply to have access to Dad's files (and hopefully my mum's letter) under the Freedom of Information Act. The office is on the third floor of Centennial Plaza, a salmon-and-steel-coloured 1980s building squatting between commuter hubs and old fabric warehouses near Central Station. The entrance foyer is full of identical lift doors, which open and deposit you in various government departments.

As I walk into the Department of Veterans' Affairs, I face two people sitting behind desks. I can't decide who to approach, then I realise that the person on the right, sitting directly in front of the door and looking straight ahead and straight through me, is a security guard. The giveaway is the small nameplate customised with a folded strip of A4 paper saying, *Security Guard*. Just to the right of the nameplate, a miniature Australian flag is sticky-taped to the desk. The office looks like it hasn't changed much since the 80s. Apart from the Australian crest and the words 'Department of Veterans' Affairs' in bronze letters on a turquoise sea behind the desks, the decoration consists of pamphlets and posters about the services they offer and one large Australian flag standing limply at the front door. There are no windows.

I approach the woman behind the desk on the left. I ask if I can sit down and tell her I'm after information about my father and a copy of the letter my mother wrote to claim a War Widow's pension.

'Was your father on the nominal roll?' she asks.

'What's nominal mean?'

'I don't know, actually.'

'Does it mean he has died, or he was conscripted?'

'I'm not sure. Hold on, I'll go and ask someone.'

She leaves the office through a door behind the security guard. I look around me. Is this a stage set for a Beckett play? Is this meant to look like the back entrance to the Department of Defence? I feel as if I've stepped back in time, as if beyond the walls, where the woman has gone, is the 'front entrance' set, full of plush carpets, the latest technology, designer furniture and shiny busy people.

After the security guard and I have sat together in silence for five minutes, an elderly couple enter stage left. He looks about ninety, still tall but stooped, and rail thin. He is dressed in light blue trousers, belted up high (in the over-stomach rather than under-stomach position), and a white shirt. She is short, up to his armpits, and not quite as old as him. She looks Japanese.

The security guard says to them, 'Won't be long. Take a seat.'

The man's voice seems to have only one volume – extremely loud.

'Veterans' Affairs!' he declares. 'Travel Pass! Have you got every-thing you need?' he asks his companion.

'Yes ... I should think so.'

I turn to look at them. His companion faces straight ahead, either looking at me or through me. I don't have my glasses on, so I can't tell.

After a little while the man declares, 'I'll be glad not to have to go out in that sun again. Too strong!'

'You shouldn't have to,' she replies.

They resume their silence.

I am facing the office woman's empty seat, looking at the Australian coat of arms on the wall behind it. The kangaroo and emu hold a shield with six little sections. She's been gone about ten minutes by now, and to kill time I started thinking about what the sections represent. Swan ... Western Australia. A red walking lion ... ? Then I begin wondering what war the old man had fought in. WWII? Part of the occupying forces in Japan, maybe? Is that where he met the woman? He looks too old for Vietnam and she doesn't look Vietnamese. My dad would have been about his age by now, and he was in Japan before Vietnam. I browse the brochures on the desk: War Graves, Mental Health Assistance, Anzac things. Why does he have to come in to renew a travel pass? Then I hear, 'Hooray!'

(It is the old man. I wonder if he is being facetious.)

'Hooray!'

(About how long he has to wait.)

'Hooray!'

After the third Hooray, I turn around, expecting to find the man with his arms raised above his head in celebration, or see him standing on his feet. Instead, he is in his chair, head slumped forward, almost touching his thighs. Asleep. His companion is still looking straight ahead. He falls silent again and only then do I realise that there'd been a *hip-hip*'s gap between each Hooray.

The DVA woman returns.

'Ok, I've scanned your ID,' she says. 'We're going digital.'

'Oh great.'

'So, I'll put in the form and it should take about thirty days for the folders to arrive here and then you can come in and go through them and copy what you like.'

'Great. Thanks. How will I know when they are here?'

'We'll send you a letter.'

'A letter? In the post?'

'Yes.'

'So not totally digital then?'

'Ha! No. Wait, I'll write your email down on the back of the form too.'

A photo of Uncle Ted

When we were kids, Mum had a friend called Aunty Ron. We visited her once every month or so. She wasn't a real aunty, just a friend of Mum's we were told to call Aunty. Her place was in Strathfield and all her upholstery was covered in plastic. Each time we drove to her house, we had to pass a church with burnt and bubbled orange glass in the windows of the steeple. Each time we drove past it, I would call out, 'The church is on fire! The church is on fire!'

Aunty Ron was tiny, not much more than five feet. She had a bowl cut, big eyes and a rounded nose. She was like a slightly larger version of the gnomes who cheerfully pushed barrows and leant against poles in her manicured front garden. Her husband, Uncle Ted, was tiny too. He smoked a pipe, wore his trousers belted up under his armpits and always smiled. He had misty grey-green eyes, the colour of the sky, far out at sea, on a stormy afternoon.

I once ate so many chips at a party at Aunty Ron's that I threw up what was essentially a packet and a half of partly digested Smiths on her beige carpet. She was never really warm to me after that. She'd sit me out in her garage and give me tubs of Play Doh to play with. If it was punishment, it didn't matter. I loved the smell of Play Doh. I'd take it out of the tub and roll it around in my hands, holding the soft, coloured blob up to my nose and breathing in the sweet scent of it.

After Uncle Ted died, Aunty Ron went to Circular Quay with a friend one day. While she was there a seagull flew down and hovered in front of her face. It hovered so long that she managed to get her camera out and take a photo of it. She was convinced it was Uncle Ted in bird form. He had been in the navy and she was near the water. She had the photo of the hovering gull framed and hung it on her loungeroom wall, along with the other photos of her family.

As a way of putting off working, I take a wander around the Australian War Memorial collection from the comfort of my home, via their website. I have information about where my dad was and when, but he's nowhere to be found on the War Memorial site. *Sorry no results found.* I feel like I'm playing *Where's Wally?*

This is the information about my dad leaving for Vietnam:
> To HQ Aust Army Force (Increment for Exercise 'Round Up')
> 5/5/65 RO ST364
> Unit Now HQ AAFV as Clerk (GD)ECN233 5/5/65 RO ST400
> Oseas Empl RICHMOND 1/6/65
> Last port of call Townsville
> Depl Saigon

Empl, I think, means emplane. I'd never heard that word before. It means *to board a plane*, similar to embark, *to board a ship*.

I find what I think is a relevant diary: The Commander's Diaries of Headquarters Australian Army Force Vietnam from 1 Dec 1965 to 31 December 1965, which include the Narrative, Duty Officer's Logs.[6] There are so many acronyms and abbreviations in them, it's like reading Morse code. After a while though, things come into focus. The day-to-day reporting of army logistics includes descriptions of the usual annoyances that would happen in any workplace.

On 11–12 December 1965, for instance, not much happened. It looks like, for the first half of the night, someone is asking the duty driver to report to Tu Xuong and they say they have reported.

For the second half of the night, from 2am until 8am, someone from Platypus reports every two hours that there is nothing to report. N.T.R.

DUTY OFFICER. Maj. QUEALY...... ....MOUNTED 0830 Hrs. 11 Dec 65. DISMOUNTED..0830 12 Dec 65....

Date/Time	Sig Phone SDS	Event	Action	Disposal
XX 112230	Phone	From GSO2 - Duty Dvr to report to TU XUONG.	Duty Dvr reported	
112300	Phone	From GSO2 - Duty Dvr to report to TU XUONG	Duty Dvr reported	
112400	Phone	From GSO2 - Duty Dvr to report to TU XUONG	Duty Dvr reported	
120215	Phone	From PLATYPUS SITREP NTR		
120400	Phone	From PLATYPUS SITREP NTR		
120600	Phone	From PLATYPUS SITREP NTR		
120805	Phone	From PLATYPUS SITREP NTR		

The next day there's a clutch problem on a truck, something from 1RAR about pay requirements, something about R&R in Bangkok for WO2 SPY and something through signals from 161 Recce Flt Damaged AC Birdstrike.

On the 17th there's a verbal message from US Maj about when flags should be put up and lowered:

Date/Time	Sig Phone SDS	Event	Action	Disposal
171755H	Verbal	Msg from US Maj to the effect that flag should be taken down daily at the fol timings :- put up a. 0800 hrs b. Lowered 1800 hrs	Lowered flag 171800 hrs and raised it at 180800 hrs.	DAAG HQ Comdt

Over the next few days there's a phone ringing in DAAGS office and the door is locked so the duty officer is unable to answer it. The hotline goes out, someone from 1RAR's mother is very ill and the family doctor has called asking for the soldier to return home. AHQ request confirmation if presence of soldier may have life-saving effect on mother's condition. On 18th December the soldier with the sick mother is told to report in uniform the next morning, in case approval is given for him to leave, and the new curfew hours are to be promulgated. Promulgate … I've come across that word a few times now. *To announce, to officially put a law into effect.*

There's no more about the soldier with the sick mother after that. He is left hanging in his uniform waiting to see if his emergency leave is approved (and they call these records narratives).

DUTY OFFICER. Capt. QUAIL ....MOUNTED. 0830 hrs 18 Dec 65.... DISMOUNTED. 0830 hrs 19 Dec 65 (Sheet 3)

Date/Time	Sig Phone SDS	Event	Action	Disposal
190400H	Phone	1 RAR – Line check – Nothing to report		GSO 2
190600H	"	1 RAR – Line check – Nothing to report		GSO 2
190800H	–	FOR ONCOMING DUTY OFFICER		
		The fol matters are outstanding.		
		(a) Maps – see separate note.		
		(b) Emergency leave S sgt GORDON. We are waiting for approval from AHQ. Member to report to you at 0900H in uniform ready to move by courier if approval given. He can be paid at same time as AATTV pers. I will be here at 0945 to take over local purchase monies. Mob 3s and pers docus to be arranged by you.		
		(c) I understand new curfew hours apply tonight. Action required to confirm and promulgate.		

A few days later, 27 December, it's as though Maj Hinds had better ways to spend his time than typing up the minutiae of army life.

DUTY OFFICER .....M.AJ...H.iN.D.S...........

Date/Time	Sig Phone SDS	Ev
		N.T.R

0.83. 27 Dec. DISMOUNTED 28083

	Action	Disposal

As I look through these diaries, set out in tables showing date and time/mode of communication (signals/phone SDS) Event, Action, Disposal, with a remark required every two hours, I wonder whether it was preferable to have days with absolutely nothing to report except N.T.R. every two hours or whether it was preferable to have action, good or bad.

N.T.R. #2

A lot of days are N.T.R. It's a handy acronym.

'How's your writing going?' a friend might ask me.

'N.T.R.'

The N.T.R. days of my life aren't necessarily bad though. I went to the doctor a few months ago for a routine pap smear and received a call from her a few days later telling me I have the strains of the HPV virus that are associated with Cervical Cancer (why did I just give those words capital letters?)

I had to see a specialist for a biopsy of my cervix – a colposcopy. I lay on the specially designed short bed (a U-shaped gap at the end and footrests either side of a large lamp), waiting for the procedure. Someone must have asked if I minded a student being in the room and I must have agreed, because at some point before everyone got to work, a tall smiling man with a large beard and bright orange turban entered the room, nodded to me and headed to see my cervix. He and the other doctor were down there conferring. I could hardly see them because of the sheet over my knees. When they both popped their heads up, it looked like I'd given birth to them – a mismatched set of medical twins.

During the colposcopy, I suggested to the main doctor they have a TV on the ceiling to distract patients, like my dentist does. He laughed, agreed it was a good idea, then asked me if I wanted to see my cervix.

'NO. Thank you!' was my first response, but as the team talked about which bits they were going to cut out, my eyes couldn't help but drift over to the screen that they were looking at, to see inside myself, to see what they were doing.

I told my partner, Adam, about it later.

What's it look like?' he asked.

'Somewhere between a throat and an arsehole,' I replied.

I've been back for another appointment since then and the doctor pulled out a little square pad printed with pictures of the female anatomy – well the reproductive part anyway.

It was headed *Female Reproductive Organs*, with the subtitle, *Patient Education Aid*. The parts of the Female Reproductive Organs were labelled: *Fallopian Tube, Uterus, Ovary, Cervix* and *Vagina*. It had never occurred to me before how much E.T. looks like the female reproductive organs.

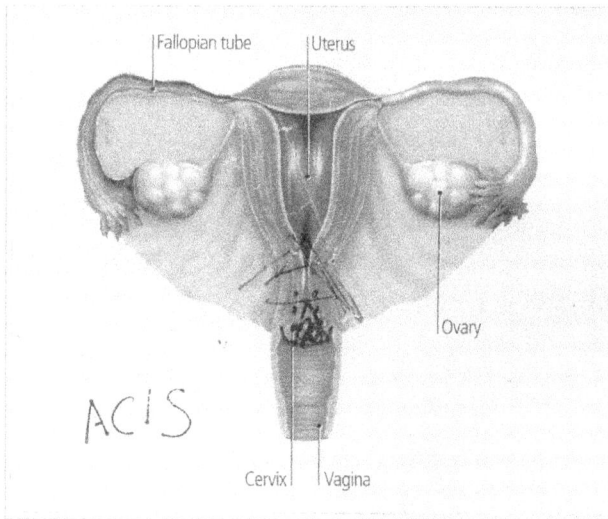

The doctor wrote ACIS on the picture and drew a little triangle on the bit they were going to have to cut out because they found precancerous cells in funny places.

They were going to do a cone biopsy. If they found anything cancerous, I'd need to have a hysterectomy. If not, I'd get to keep my parts intact.

My psyche must have overheard that I couldn't have sex for a month after the operation because I was suddenly plump with hormones. I felt so fecund that I did a pregnancy test even though I was fifty-three and hadn't had a regular period for two years.
Everything about me felt ripe and hungry. What was going on?

I asked if I could postpone the operation until after I'd done another stint of work in Arnhem Land. The doctors conferred.

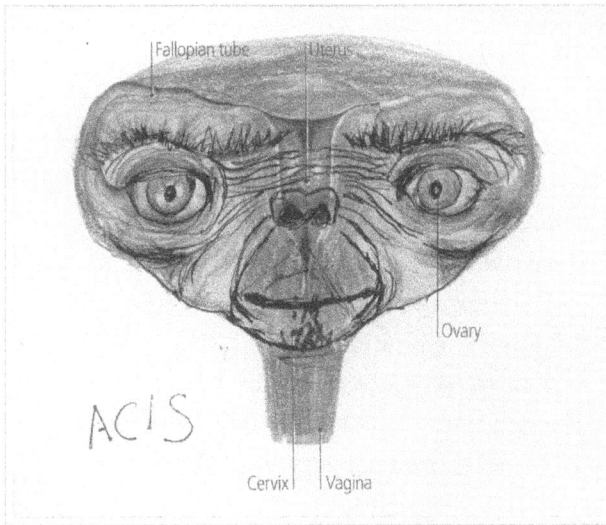

'Obviously,' I pointed out, 'if there's any health implications from delaying the surgery, I won't go.' The nice doctor came in and told me he'd looked at my pictures again and it was fine to postpone the surgery a month. I really would have preferred an N.T.R. result from my test, but there you had it. I was on the fate train and it would take me where it wanted to go.

A uterus picture and a passport

I had filled out a form and emailed it to the army asking for copies of my father's service records. I scanned the form and my birth certificate at the library and emailed them to make the request. Now I've just been told that I need to provide a copy of my father's death certificate and a copy of my identity papers, such as a passport or driver's licence that has my signature on it.

I understand that the Department of Veterans' Affairs is a different department to the Department of Defence, but wouldn't a soldier's widow, having been granted a War Widow's pension, be proof enough of the death of that soldier? I feel like emailing documents from the Department of Veterans' Affairs to the Army Records Department – ones where they have stamped the front page 'Deceased' and ones where their internal reports say my dad's early death had nothing to do with his war service – but I don't. I just copy what I think they want and send that via email.

I have to scan the documents at the library. I scan my passport and my uterus diagram at the same time. The lady from the library hovers nearby to assist me. I try very hard not to let her see my uterus.

What would she make of that?

Deceased

The first time I speak to Denise about the night Dad died, thirty-eight years later

'What do you remember about that night he died?'

'Not a lot, to be honest. All I remember is, I remember that I saw him just before I went to bed. We passed in the hallway. Then all I remember is a tearful thing around the dining room table where Mum told us that he'd died. That's very vague, I must say. And I remember that she made a joke about how now she'd be able to get rid of the Morris Minor sitting in the yard. That was about the only thing I remember. And I remember having to call her friend, you know, Jean from Punchbowl. She made me call up and tell them that Dad had died, so ... that was a bit hard.'

'You had to do that?'

'Yeah, I had to call them up. And I remember both of us not being allowed to go to the funeral. So, I stayed at home with you for that.'

'I wonder if that was because you had to look after me?'

'Probably, I think, but I'm not sure. At the time I thought it was because, ah ... I didn't think about that aspect. It was only yesterday when you mentioned it, I thought, "Oh, that's why ..." You know the funniest thing, the thing that also stuck in my memory is that, at that time, I can't remember exactly which day, I opened the front door and there was this little puppy or small dog that came to the door. It was just playing and being really friendly at the front door and then it went away.' She laughs. 'I always thought, *That's weird*. It was just like some sort of reincarnation of Dad, in puppy form, appeared at the door. It was actually really ... it was weird. Seriously weird. Like, there's this friendly dog, it appeared and then it went away again.'

'And that was it?'

'I'm not ... I mean ... I don't believe in the afterworld ... but it was like, *I'm not into this weird stuff* ... but ... like ... that was weird.

And anyway, that's pretty much all I remember. But I do know that afterwards I found out that he'd been sent a letter by his doctor or something telling him that if he didn't improve things, he was going to die. So, he knew that beforehand and he'd just started on a diet and was on a quitting smoking thing at the beginning of that year. So, it lasted about a month before he died. And then, after he died, Mum found ... he'd kept all the letters that she'd sent him and then she ripped them all up and threw them out. I just managed to get one and I kept that.'

'I've got that actually.'

'Yeah, but there were lots of other ones, that she ripped up and threw out.'

'And the letters that he wrote her? She just ... ? Because ... you know ... you've got that letter from her to him ...'

'... he didn't talk much ... obviously.'

'No.'

'The most he ever talked, apart from when he was explaining cars – I was probably the only female learner driver who could explain perfectly how a clutch worked – was when I sat him down and talked to him about his family history, and then he was really chatty. He told me a lot of things. He knew the number plates of every car that he'd ever had, and all of his jobs and everything. Actually, when you made an effort to talk to him, he would talk to you, but I think he went through life with us, I just ... I don't know ...'

'Enduring it?'

'Probably. He was a very interesting man, you know. I think ... He knew everything. You know? And he would do everything for you. I mean ... sorry ... I'm starting to cry now ...'

'Oh ... sorry ...'

'Yeah, because ... you know ... he'd always take me to hockey matches. He'd always have a chat with me. He'd have a comment on the game. He just did it without making a fuss.'

'But did he come and watch you? I don't ever remember him watching my games.'

'Yeah, he came. He'd drive the car, then he'd sit there and watch from his car or something. He didn't make a big fuss about coming up and standing on the sidelines. But he was very supportive, you know. When we had to learn our times tables, I always remember that he made these times tables on cardboard and he put them in plastic sandwich bags, so we had a flip thing we could learn our times tables from. If you ever had a question, you could always go and ask him, and he'd always be able to tell you things. And I remember that was the time that it hit me when he died, because he died so suddenly … and because I was away from home … so … I went back and pretended that it never happened. But then you just sit there and one day you think, *I'll ask Dad that* and then you think, *oh actually, I can never ask him again.*'

Before and after

You know those questionnaires where adults are asked what advice they'd give their teenage self? I wonder what advice I'd give my teenage self. It depends when I was giving it, I guess. Before or after. My life was cleaved in two at fifteen.

The time before, everything was a given. How things were was how they were meant to be. Is that how all kids feel? Seeing as it's the only world you know, you make sense of it with whatever facts or directions your parents give you.

Before, I had a mum and a dad who loved each other. Dad would make my mum poached eggs on toast and cups of tea in the morning. Mum would make Dad dinner and keep it hot on top of a simmering saucepan when he was late home from work. We'd watch TV while we ate dinner at the table. I found inventive ways to avoid eating Mum's bad cooking. We wrapped our dinner scraps in newspaper. My sisters and I took turns at washing and drying up. On Friday nights, Mum would open a bottle of Sparkling Starwine or Passion Pop and have a glass or two in front of the TV. Dad would come home a bit tipsy from the RSL, try to hug her and she'd bat him away saying, 'Stop that. Stop that. Go away.'

When we weren't at the table eating, everyone retreated to themselves. Dad would be in the garage, Mum would be in the garden, Denise would have her head in a book and Maree would be out or in her room. I had to find something to kill the time. I'd bounce a ball over and over, marvelling at the physics of it (what makes it bounce back time and again?). Or I'd roller-skate up and down our driveway, trying to lift one leg up behind myself elegantly, and finish with a pirouette. I'd look into Mum's dressing-table mirror and arrange the two moveable wings so I could form a thousand visions of myself disappearing into infinity.

I did this regularly, with an almost autistic intensity.

What would I say to the before child?

Maybe, 'Enjoy the boring bits while they last.'

Maybe, 'Spend more time with your dad.'

After. My sisters had moved out. It was me and Mum in an empty house. I don't remember much. We watched a lot of TV.

Prisoner

The Restless Years

Number 96

The Love Boat

The Young Doctors

The Sullivans

A Country Practice

We watched Molly from *A Country Practice* die. In the final scene of the season, the camera cut between Molly lying on a couch, her husband and daughter in a field flying a kite, and the kite's smiling face dancing in an overcast sky. The husband looks at Molly, smiles and waves. She smiles and waves back. There's a shot of the smiling kite in the sky, then a few more shots alternating between Molly watching and the husband and child flying the kite. Then (we all knew it was coming) a shot of the husband as he looks towards Molly. He hesitates, drops the kite string and runs towards the camera. The screen fades to black as we hear him yelling, 'Molly!' The end.[7]

We cried more then, sitting in front of the TV watching Molly die, than we cried together about my dad.

Life with Birds #3

Mrs Kendrick lived on the downhill side of us with her daughter Carmel and Jangles, the Budgie. Mrs Kendrick had a stroke in her forties. For twenty years she sat in a chair in her house and watched TV, watched North Ryde life pass by her window or spoke to Jangles. Watching North Ryde life pass by, during the week, was essentially watching the lady across the road come out in her brunch coat around 11am to check her letterbox or watching one or other of the identical Woods twins riding past on their ten-speed racer, to or from the corner shops after school. They were so identical, if you didn't know they were twins, you'd think it was just the one restless boy.

Mrs Kendrick could move around all right, not enough to go out by herself, but enough to get up and go to the toilet or change the channel on the TV. Her mind was still lively though. She could understand everything that was said to her, she just couldn't say anything besides, 'One two.'

When Carmel was at work, Mum would often say to me, *Go next door and see if Mrs Kendrick needs anything, would you, like a good girl.* I'd go, resenting Mum's habit of asking me to do everything *like a good girl.* What does that even mean?

I'd get to their back door, knock and let myself in. Sometimes the exchanges were short: 'Hi, Mrs Kendrick, how are you?'

'One two,' she'd say, slowly shaking her head and giving the words a feeble edge.

'Mum says do you need anything?'

'One two,' she'd say, shaking her head for *No.*

'Ok. Bye then.'

Sometimes, I'd stay a bit longer. If I arrived at her back door and she called out, 'One two!' before I could get in, I knew it meant that her bird Jangles was loose, and I should be careful getting through the door. She liked to let him fly around the house. He'd sit on her shoulder, peck her on the lips, shuffle across behind her head to the other shoulder, take off, fly around and land back on her shoulder. They watched TV together. She had taught Jangles to talk and he said, 'One two,' as well.

'Do you need anything today?'

'One two,' she replied with an enthusiastic nod, pointing her finger towards the road. I looked across the road and couldn't see anything, so I looked back to her. 'One two,' she pointed again, this time clearly at the letterbox.

'Oh, should I see if there's any mail?'

'One two,' she nodded. I went out the front of her house to check and returned.

'Sorry, there's nothing there today.'

'One two,' she shrugged, with a tone of thanks and goodbye.

'Ok, see ya.'

I often thought about Mrs Kendrick. I tried to imagine what she must have been like before it happened, when she was one of the top legal secretaries in Sydney, with four kids and a husband. She'd spent the twenty years since, in the same house, in the same chair. Wouldn't you go crazy? But Mrs Kendrick's eyes were bright. With Jangles on her shoulder, jumping up on to the top of her head, shuffling back and forth, his claws getting stuck in her hair, she came alive, chuckling as he flew off, shitting on something and bumping into light fittings.

'One two,' she'd say to me, smiling and pointing at him.

'One two.'

More regretful sales

Hello everyone,

I am looking at giving my Sulphur up for adoption. A very long story short, my wife and I have split up and I can no longer give her (my sulphur) what she needs/deserves (you all have probably heard this a million times).

She is about 4yrs old, I've had her for about two years (she was mistreated at her previous home from people that had no patience). Very friendly and affectionate.

I don't want to give her up but if I can find a better home where she can get the attention she needs, then I'll give her up, otherwise she will stay with me. I live in Perth and will only adopt her to someone I can meet in person.

Summary

Beautiful African grey parrot, he is approx. 6 years old, we have had him 2 years.

Description

He can say quite a few sayings, where's mummies boy, love you, Ba ba black sheep, good night, good morning etc.

He is better with men than women, he does come out of his cage but rarely flys around. He does bite when in his cage as this is his domain.

He will come with his cage which is a corner cage with 2 bowls on top for when he comes out, it has a removable top tray and also a removable bottom tray.

All his toys etc Reason for sale I cannot give him the time he needs now as I work long hours and he's not keen on my partner.

I can send him interstate.

[Source: gumtree.com.au]

My big christening

I was christened under duress when I was fourteen years old. Denise got christened too. She was seventeen. Mum was hedging her bets. In case it was true, she wanted whoever was in charge to recognise us when we got to Heaven and to let us in. This was before Dad died, not long before though, so perhaps she felt change was on its way. She had us christened in the simple white church her father helped build in Quandialla, where she grew up. Our christening coincided with the anniversary of the church being built. All her family would be there.

Mum wasn't that religious. She only went to church for weddings, funerals or performances of Handel's *Messiah* at Easter. She persuaded/bribed us to be christened by promising us outfits – nice new outfits we could be christened in. After much looking around, I chose a pale pink batik twin-set with green leaf patterns on it. The skirt had splits up the side and a scalloped hem. The top had drawstrings on the shoulders. I wore a choker of small shells. Denise also went for batik, a simple white shift dress with flowers on it and a drawstring waist. She wore a brown jumper over the top to counteract any possible prettiness.

Neither of us realised, when we agreed to be christened, that we'd have to do anything other than get a bit of water poured on our heads. We didn't expect that we'd be taken into the priest's back room together and questioned about our faith or about the conversations we'd had with our local minister. The priest sported an ill-fitting ginger wig. It was as if he'd found a fox dead by the side of the road, chopped off its tail and head, scooped out the innards, then popped it on his head. The fact that he had no visible eyebrows did not help his cause.

We didn't have any faith, of course, unless you count faith in music or boys or looking good in batik. We had to lie. We had to look the priest in the eye (rather than at the wig) and talk to him about our love of Jesus.

When we walked back out to the crowd, we searched for our mum, so we could glare at her. During the ceremony we had to stand at the front of the humble wooden church, with our backs to the congregation, and repeat things after the priest. Denise went first. He said things about Faith and Jesus and Sins. She repeated things about Faith and Jesus and Sins. He asked her to bend over and poured Holy Water over her head. The water went over her face and into her eyes. She wasn't allowed to wipe it off.

When I started giggling, Denise looked at me, through the Holy Water, with a brand of sisterly rage I hadn't seen before. I don't know if anyone else knew I was laughing except Mum, who told me later she could see my shoulders shaking from where she sat. I had my turn next and then, when we thought it was all over, we were shuffled outside for photos with the priest. I still have the photos – us in front of the little white church, either side of the priest, squinting into the sun, at either Mum or Dad. The priest has his arms around us. You can see the imprints on our skin where he is holding us just a bit too tight.

Dad died less than a year later. After he died, Mum gave up on religion altogether.

'I don't want to believe in a God that would do that to me,' she said.

What advice would I give to that 'after' girl?
I don't know.
I'd tell her I'm sorry she felt so alone.
I'd tell her things will turn out OK.
I'd tell her people do the best they can.

Family secrets (that I know about) #1 – Dad's secret book

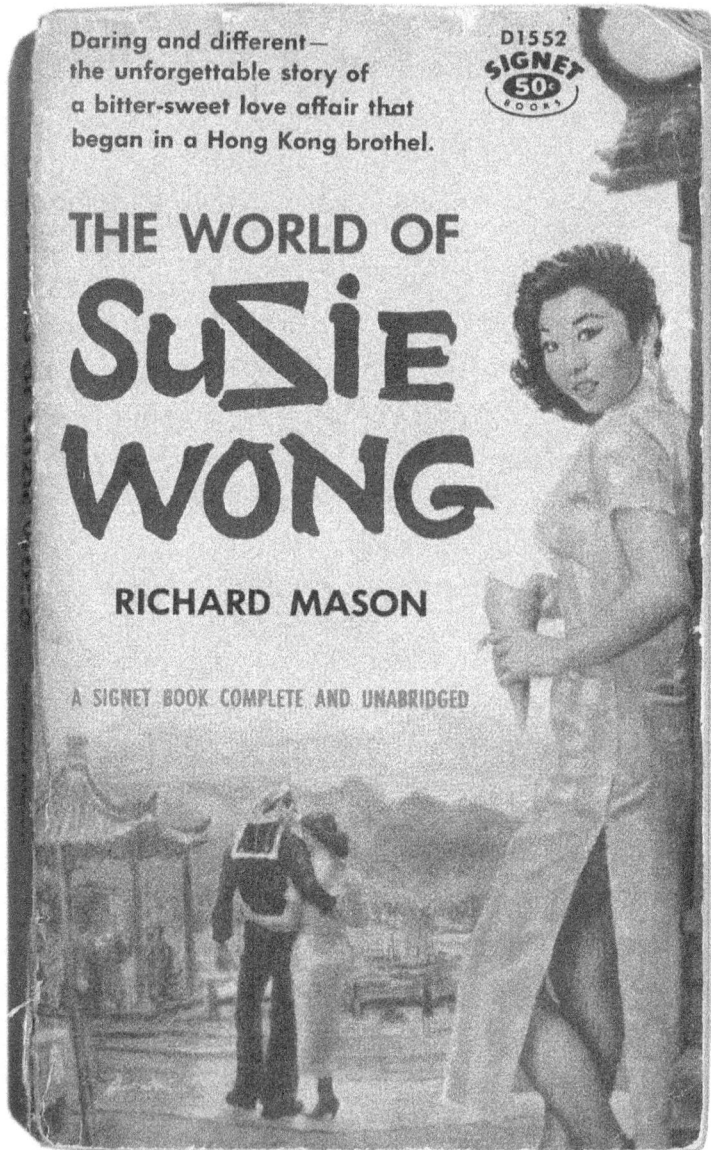

Daring and different—
the unforgettable story of
a bitter-sweet love affair that
began in a Hong Kong brothel.

D1552

SIGNET
50¢
BOOKS

THE WORLD OF
SuSie WONG

RICHARD MASON

A SIGNET BOOK COMPLETE AND UNABRIDGED

PEACE FROM NERVOUS SUFFERING

DR CLAIRE WEEKES

a practical, everyday guide
to understanding, confidence
and recovery

The angry pages

I have been angry for weeks now. My brain is like a clenched fist inside my head.

1.

As promised, Veterans' Affairs have looked through their files. Instead of writing me a letter to inform me that the documents were ready (as they said they would), I received, via registered post, a package of the documents they had copied. After I picked them up from the post office, I bought myself a coffee, took it all to the park, sat on the grass and opened the envelope.

> *Dear Ms Rennex ... You have been granted access ... following are the copies ... Why do you consider that service caused, contributed to, or if applicable, aggravated the incapacity(ies) that led to death (supporting documentary evidence may be attached) ... see attached statement ...*

I found it. I found the letter Mum wrote to claim a War Widow's pension. But the person who copied it didn't get it all on the page. The sides have been cut off, as has the bottom.

I would have thought, if a daughter was asking for a copy of the letter her mother wrote to claim a War Widow's pension, the least the person copying it could do would be to get the whole (fucking) thing on the page. Isn't that one of those jobs that you might want to tiptoe a bit carefully around? Not just slap something on the copier while you stare out of the window thinking about lunch?

2.

When I was telling my friend Kay how full-on work had been, she looked at a Facebook page on her phone and said, 'Look, here's a lost puppy. Isn't he cute? Maybe you should have him?'

'What's that got to do with what I was saying?'

'I don't know, but look at him.'

'But he's somebody's dog.'

'But he's cute.'

3.

Along with the badly photocopied letter, I got copies of a whole lot of medical files on my dad. As I browsed through them, my image of him changed ... irrevocably. As I read through Dad's records, he became more and more ... ordinary.

He tried to get into the navy but got rejected because he had bad teeth.

He was obese.

He had VD.

He smoked too much.

He fell over carrying a big box of papers.

The box fell on top of him and he hurt his back.

4.

3pm. Time to watch Judge Judy. She's angry too. She doesn't tolerate fools. It makes me feel better.

5.

Because they did such a bad job of photocopying, I went back to the Veterans' Affairs office to look through the actual files. I found Mum's letter but marked a whole lot of other stuff I wanted to have copied too. Stuff they hadn't previously thought I'd be interested in, stuff that was actually as interesting as Mum's letter (which I photographed on my phone because I didn't trust them to photocopy it properly a second time). The security guard that day had very long fake nails, which would definitely be problematic if trouble broke out.

I shuffled through the folders. As I got further down the pile, I saw the police report to the coroner about my dad … and one or two lines about there being recently digested food in his stomach … no … not reading any further on that one. I tagged it to request a copy and figured I'd revisit that when I got less angry.

Do I really want to know this stuff?

6.

Is it just me, or are Myna birds acting strange lately? I walked outside the other day to find two pairs of them doing what looked like cavorting in the middle of the road outside my house. I walked right near them and they didn't move. All Myna birds are looking a lot bolder. I followed some particularly bold ones and filmed them on my phone.

7.

I just phoned Veterans' Affairs. The files I left there three weeks ago to get copied haven't been copied. I'm told it will take thirty days.

'We'll need to order them in.'

'But you've got the files there.'

'I'll need to talk to Linda and she's at lunch.'

'No, you've got them there. I spoke to someone. They just need to be copied.'

A woman called Kathy calls back. She's spoken to Linda. She explains they'd just been sitting around because the person who was meant to do them had a car accident and hadn't been in the office. Kathy says she'll do them. When she calls back to say they are done, I ask whether she copied the whole letter that my mother had written to claim a War Widow's pension. She checks.

'The letter is foolscap. It didn't fit on an A4 page.'

'I don't mind if it's over two pages.'

'Well, it's just a few lines at the bottom that were missing.'

'But that's why I went back into the office, because I wanted a copy of the whole letter.'

'Well, we can only do what's physically possible.'

'But you can copy it on two pages. You know, the top half on one and the bottom ...'

'I know,' she said, 'but the second page will only have one or two lines.'

'I don't care. I requested the whole letter. I don't mind if it's on two pages. I just want the whole thing. OK?'

'I'll see what I can do. I'll send it out in the post tomorrow. But the second page is only going to have one or two lines on it ...'

8.
Am I going mad?

9.
Brother printers don't supply the cable that connects your printer to your computer.

10.

I try to download the printer driver software five times, then ring for help. The young man on the *Brother* technical helpline says 'helpful' things like the forward slash is on the same key as the question mark.

10a.

Maybe I should have used bullet points.

11.

Did I really just have that argument about photocopying with the woman in Veterans' Affairs?

12.

People who I want to tell to go fuck themselves:

    Everyone at work.

    Couples who walk along King St slowly, holding hands.

    The people who rented my neighbours' place and are shouting.

    Slow drivers.

    The woman at Veterans' Affairs who can't photocopy.

    Medicare.

    Officeworks.

    Brother.

    The rain.

13.

People who I don't want to tell to go fuck themselves:

My sister Denise, who loves family history and has an enquiring science-y mind and always shares some little thought or insight, like telling me that the iron in our bodies comes from exploded supernovas – not just any old stars but specifically supernovas. And that Dad had a secret book in the bottom of his wardrobe called *The World of Suzy Wong*, about a Chinese sex worker in Hong Kong with a heart of gold who falls for an ex-serviceman. The year Denise took it on holidays to read, Aunty Mary was horrified and asked her if she really should be reading 'that'.

Dogs.

Babies.

14.

My father's recently digested stomach contents have been sitting in an envelope on a chair in the kitchen for a week now.

15.

The second lot of photocopies arrived. Inside is a copy of the police report to the coroner on my dad's death. There's also an A4 page with Mum's letter claiming a War Widow's pension. Attached to the copy is a yellow sticky note.

In my opinion my Husband's relatively early death is a justification for this application for the War widows pension.

I believe he suffered considerable stress not only during but after his term of service in Vietnam which changed his life and ours considerably.

Prior to his service in Vietnam, my husband was a loving outgoing type of person, who enjoyed good health and a happy family life.

On his return the change in his disposition was evident. While his attitude to others seemingly remained unchanged, it was evident to me (his wife) that he was greatly disturbed.

The close communicative relationship we enjoyed before his departure had changed considerably, he became quite withdrawn, he refused absolutely to speak of his term in Vietnam, and our everyday problems were left for me to resolve.

His inability to sleep at night was further evidence of the stress he was suffering, and as a result of this he began smoking heavily, and that in turn caused persistent coughing, which distressed him greatly. He was advised by the Dr. many times to stop smoking, and although he wanted to, seemed unable.

In his last years my Husband suffered recurring pains in his arms, and to the best of my knowledge the Dr was treating this as Rheumatism, there was never any mention to me of the possibility of heart trouble which made his sudden death so hard to come to terms with.

My Husband's greatest wish was that our Daughters should be given the opportunity of a tertiary Education, and for this reason I returned to work as soon as I was able, to ease the financial pressure this would create. However his untimely death has placed great strain on me, in as much as I still have two daughters dependent on me, one at University and one at High School, who this year will be going to University.

I trust my request will be given favourable consideration.

Yours E. Rennex

DEPARTMENT OF VETERANS' AFFAIRS

P.O. Box 3994
Sydney 2001

New South Wales Branch
77 York Street Sydney 2000
STD Code 02 Telephones 2 0234 Ext.7477

60

57

In my opinion my husband's relatively early death is
justification for this application as a disabled pension.
I believe his suffered considerable stress not only during,
but after his term of service in Vietnam which changed
his life and ours considerably.

Prior to his service in Vietnam, my husband was a
loving outgoing type of person, who enjoyed good health
and a happy family life.

On his return the change in his disposition was
evident. While his attitude to others seemingly remained
unchanged, it was evident to me (his wife) that he
was greatly disturbed.

The close communications relationship we enjoyed
before his departure had changed considerably, he became
quite withdrawn, he refused absolutely to speak of his term
in Vietnam, and our every day problems were left for me
to resolve.

His inability to sleep at night was further evidence of the
stress he was suffering, and as a result of this he began
smoking heavily, and that in turn caused persistent
coughing, which distressed him greatly. He was advised
by the Dr. many times to stop smoking, and although
he wanted to, seemed unable.

In his last year my husband suffered recurring
pains in his arms, and to the best of my knowledge the Dr.
was treating this as Rheumatism, there was never any
mention to me of the possibility of heart trouble which made
his sudden death so hard to come to terms with.

My husband's greatest wish was that our daughters should
be given the opportunity of a tertiary education, and for this
reason I returned to work as soon as I was able, to ease
the financial pressures this would create, however his untimely
death has placed a great strain on me, as much as I
still had two daughters dependent on me, one at the university
and one at High School, who this year will be going to University.

I trust my request will be given favourable consideration.

Yours E. Lennox

HI BRONWYN

THIS PAGE HAS
BEEN MINIMISED
TO FIT ENTIRE
LETTER

REGARDS
Kathy

Rank: CONSTABLE 1st CLASS
Annual leave from June, Dec 1980

(Continued overleaf)

NOTE: (1) This form should be prepared in quadruplicate in all cases where a death is reported to the Coroner. The original and two copies
should be forwarded to the Coroner. All statements in duplicate should be lodged with the Coroner at least 7 days before the date of

Report of death

About 11.45pm on the 23-1-80, the deceased had been watching television at home, when he went to bed where he complained to his wife of chest pains and pains in both his arms. He was also suffering hot and cold spells. He requested that his wife get his next door neighbour Mr Mullens drive him to Ryde Hospital. Whilst in Cecil Street, Ryde en route to Ryde Hospital about 1 mile away, the deceased said to Mr Mullens, "I think I'm gone mate". The deceased then started making gurgling sounds and vomited and slumped over onto Mr Mullens. The deceased arrived at Ryde Hospital at 12-05am on the 24-1-80 where attempts by hospital staff to revive him were unsuccessful and life was pronounced extinct at 12.36am that day by Dr Taylor. Prior to death, the deceased had enjoyed good health and had not suffered from any ailments apart from a weight problem. THERE ARE NO SUSPICIOUS CIRCUMSTANCES SURROUNDING THE DEATH OF JOHN RENNEX.

Honk if you are the son or daughter of a Vietnam Veteran

I was sitting at my friend Cath's kitchen table while she cooked dinner. I was staying with her while I was working nearby. She asked me what I was writing about, and as usual I jumbled out a response that didn't feel quite adequate.

'It's sort of about the impacts of war service, and our family's experience of it, but it's also about me looking back as an adult and trying to find out about my dad and filling in the gaps. It's also about suburbs and families and about the interaction between individuals and institutions. Oh, and it's also about birds.' At that point in my explanation I'd usually give up and say that I needed to work out a better pitch.

'You should speak to Colin when he gets here,' she said. 'He's a writer and his dad was a Vietnam Veteran too.'

A few days later, when Colin arrived, he came for dinner at Cath's. When he asked me about my project, I stumbled over my pitch once more, then said, 'Cath mentioned your dad was a Vietnam veteran too. I'd love to talk to you about that sometime if you wouldn't mind.' Right then and there his story came out.

He told us his dad was nineteen when his name came up in the lottery and he was conscripted. Colin was conceived after his father came back. His mother was convinced the strange rashes that broke out on his face and back throughout his childhood were a result of his dad's exposure to Agent Orange. That wasn't the only legacy of service.

The man who returned to their family was not the man who left. He was broken by the experience. He became an alcoholic. He tried to commit suicide several times when Colin was growing up but refused to see a 'psycho doctor' because he thought they were a waste of time. When his wife was struggling to deal with his behaviour, she snuck away to see a doctor in her closest town and they did offer her counselling, but it was in Sydney. She lived in the country. It might as well as have been on the moon.

Once, in an effort to speak to his dad about his war service, Colin had the photos his dad had taken there scanned and printed. He gave them to him, hoping that maybe they could talk about them. His dad refused to look at them.

We spoke about the Vietnam Veterans Family Study conducted by the Department of Veterans' Affairs between 2008 and 2016. Colin had received a letter in the post one day, inviting him to be involved. The tone of the letter was like, 'Hey come and join a gang and meet other cool people and talk about your experiences.' Colin wasn't initially going to take part but decided that, because there would be a survey, he would. He wanted his experience to be counted.

He attended a BBQ hosted by the people doing the survey and, being a vegetarian, was offered lettuce and tomato sauce on bread. At the event, one of the organisers had stickers that said:

Honk if you are the son or daughter of a Vietnam veteran.

They were bright yellow with red writing and were selling for $5 each. Colin was pretty broke at the time. He took out all the money from his pockets and counted it. He only had $4 and some change, so he couldn't afford one. At Cath's table he mimed counting out the coins in his hand and then shrugging and putting them back in his pockets and looking a bit sad.

'You know the thing that makes me angry?' he said. 'They asked us all these questions and then they told us it was so that they could do things better in the future. They didn't want to do anything for us. They just wanted to study us. We provided them with statistics. Didn't you get a letter inviting you to take part?' he asked.

'No. I didn't. Maybe they couldn't find me.'

'The organisation still exists,' he said, 'though I think they changed the name of it, changed the letters around or something.' He googled *Sons and Daughters of Vietnam Veterans*. 'Oh,' he said when he found the site. After a few beats, he grimaced then read out the contents on the first page.

The Vietnam Veterans' Sons & Daughters Support Programme (VVSDSP) assists eligible children of Vietnam Veterans who have one of the following conditions:
>   spina bifida manifesta
>   cleft lip
>   cleft palate
>   adrenal gland cancer
>   acute myeloid leukaemia.[8]

'I consider myself one of the lucky ones,' he said.

HONK
IF YOU'RE
HORNY!

HONK
IF YOU

HONKY
TONK
GILMER, TEXAS   WWW.HONKYTONKTEXAS.US

HONK IF YOU
DON'T EXIST

HONK IF YOU'RE
BORING

HONK IF YOU HAVE TO
POOP

HONK IF YOU LOVE
DYING AND BEING DEAD

HONK IF YOU ARE A
FUCKING IDIOT

HONK IF YOU ARE
LOSING YOUR MIND

HONK IF YOU LOVE JESUS
TEXT IF YOU WANT TO MEET HIM

HONK IF YOU
Love
Jesus

HONK IF YOU ARE
ON DRUGS

Putting bones back in a ghost

Dad was someone I hardly knew, who disappeared. First, he disappeared to Vietnam when I was a baby; then he disappeared down to his garage to hang out with his cars and tools and the company of the radio when he returned home. He completed his act of disappearance in 1980 in the middle of the night.

With his perpetual cigarettes, I may as well write him in smoke.

What am I trying to do? Put bones back into a ghost? When I patch him together with health records, he is too much of a body – VD, bad teeth, sweaty feet and partly digested stomach contents. When I speak to my family, he becomes a benign smudge – a different man to each; even a different colour in death. When I look at old photos and sift through archives, there's too much background and not enough subject.

It's as if the shape of him is there, but not the substance. I have the world around him, and the world without him, and I have an accumulation of small losses that don't feel like they amount to much – like being stuck in a house with a heartbroken shell of a mother, or of me having to mow the front lawn on weekends along with all the other dads, while their teenage daughters (I imagined) were off having fun. It doesn't feel like a story, more like an equation. Grief came to equal retreat. I felt alone. That equation still catches me, but in reverse. Sometimes, when I'm alone, I feel the grief of that time.

Perceived burdensomeness and thwarted belongingness

I decided I wanted to find one of those stickers to send to Colin, so I started poking around online. I came across a Senate Inquiry Report made to parliament in August 2017 called *The Constant Battle: Suicide by Veterans*,[9] which considered why returned servicemen and women commit suicide at such high rates. I was struck by this point:

> The need to streamline the administrative practices of DVA was the overwhelming concern of the majority of submissions to the inquiry ... There are a complex range of services available for veterans and the committee heard that people struggle to navigate them.[10]

Even after my meagre interactions with the DVA I wasn't surprised. What was it like for veterans or their families seeking support – encountering different forms, different people, different departments? Having to explain yourself multiple times or fit your problems into bureaucratic-shaped boxes might compound whatever struggle you were facing as a result of service. It's easy to imagine that, for some, an extra phone call or required document is a bridge too far.

> Suicide Prevention Australia commented that it had 'received feedback from multiple sources that the processes involved in engaging with DVA are perceived to exacerbate veterans' stress and we posit that this may add to the perception of perceived burdensomeness and thwarted belongingness, and therefore suicide risk'.[11]

A correction from Colin

Upon reflection, after reading your story, I realised I got the name of the sticker wrong that night, which is why you weren't able to track it down. I got it confused with a bumper sticker I wrote about as part of a Uni Theatre project some years ago. That sticker was titled 'Honk If You Are On Lithium' (it was a bumper sticker available in the USA, highlighting the high rates of people diagnosed with and medicated for Bipolar Disorder). For some reason I merged that sticker with the one the 'Sons and Daughters of Vietnam Veterans' produced. I did some research and digging around online and found something resembling the bumper sticker that was available at the BBQ I went to:

Submission: Inquiry into suicide by veterans and ex-service personnel
From: John & Karen Bird (Parents of Jesse S. Bird 1RAR 8527349 – Afghanistan – Veteran) 2017[12]

Attention: Senators of the Australian Parliament

Thank you for providing us with the opportunity to record our thoughts on behalf of our family and to make a submission to the Senate Enquiry into Suicide by Veterans and ex-service Personnel.

Our son, Jesse, joined the Australian Army in 2007. He was an elite level athlete, booming with charisma and self confidence and proud to be a member of the ADF. He was deployed to Afghanistan in June of 2009 and returned to us in February 2010. The confident young man who went away – did not return the same person. Instead, Jesse returned affected by a cocktail of nightmares, anxiety, shame, remorse, damaged shoulders, self-medicating with alcohol and cigarette addiction. Told to move on and not to talk to family about his experiences, he fought his demons and he tried to settle back into life at 1RAR Townsville. Jesse's life spiralled downhill during 2011/2012 and without family support since this time, he would no doubt have become a statistic. (He had applied for some time off to seek some help privately but this was denied him by the army – he was left with no option but to resign with no plan put in place for his future).

He has been in and out of relationships and work since his self discharge from the army in 2012. Jesse has been diagnosed with PTSD – He has been endeavouring to seek assistance from DVA for the last eighteen months without success – it seems to him and us that the level of bureaucracy is intentionally obstructionist and unedifying. The jungle of paperwork, the lack of follow-up and the non-existent support has contributed to his deteriorating mental health. He is involved with VVCS and is currently involved in a 12 Week PTSD Specific Counselling program which finishes in early December. Jesse has not received any money what-so-ever from DVA or Centrelink to help him survive and without our financial and emotional help he would be on the street or worse.

This whole experience has taken a serious toll on our family. We have been self-employed business owners and employers on the Gold Coast for more than twenty five years. We have paid our taxes, and have always been 'lifters' – to coin Joe Hockey's phrase. It beggars belief to us that we can send our young men and women overseas in the defence of our nation and fail to support those who are damaged by this process. Our politicians of all persuasions, are ready to stand at attention at War Memorials around the country and lay expensive wreaths and offer platitudes in all our names whilst our suffering Veterans are screaming – some loudly but many more silently – at deaf ears for help.

This confounds us all. We say deaf ears – because surely this must be the case – because if it wasn't, 'why is all of this so'?

Thank you in anticipation of immediate change of policy
John, Karen, Brendan & Kate Bird

Suicide by veterans and ex-service personnel
Submission 317 – Supplementary Submission
Submission: Inquiry into suicide by veterans and ex-service personnel[13]

From: John & Karen Bird – Parents of recently deceased Veteran Jesse S. Bird 1 RAR 8527349 (1984–2017)

For Your Belated Attention: Senators of the Australian Parliament – August 14th 2017

It is with a heavy heart that John and I write to you this evening – the final night for lodgement of Submissions to this Senate Inquiry. Our beloved son, Jesse Stephen Bird committed suicide on June 27th 2017 using his army issued ropes and tackle. Jesse wore his favourite 1 RAR Alpha Company Spartacus jumper and prominently displayed his medals and service records for those who found him, to see. Poignantly, Jesse had surrounded himself with the rejection letters he had received from the Department of Veteran Affairs on May 8th 2017. These letters rejected Jesse's claim for assistance because his DVA accepted conditions (PTSD, Major Depressive Illness and Alcohol Abuse) were not deemed 'permanent and stable' at that time. Well, luckily for the bureaucrats at the Department of Veteran Affairs and the Doctors and Psychologists who had profited from their so-called professional treatment of our son – Jesse's conditions finally became permanent on June 27th 2017 when he ended his life. We draw to your urgent attention that Jesse had pleaded for financial assistance on June 22nd, five days prior to his suicide – 'I need real help' and 'I have done my time and I need your help please'. Jesse also stated that 'if I didn't have the support of the RSL and my friends I would have come close to becoming another suicide statistic'. He had $5.20 left in his bank account when he communicated with a faceless DVA staff member that day. Jesse believed he had received an unsympathetic hearing and lodged a complaint the same day which we believe was not actioned for seven days; two days after his death.

John and I believe that maladministration by incompetent and adversarial DVA staff contributed directly to the suicide death of our beloved Jesse. We also draw to your attention that the sum of $4551.00 was transferred by DVA into Jesse's bank account 10 days after his death and that DVA staff were supposedly communicating posthumously with him by phone on June 29th and July 19th 2017!

Jesse died on June 27th 2017 after his legitimate claims for financial help had been stonewalled for more than two years. A trail of excessive and repetitive paperwork and doctor's and psychologist's appointments led Jesse nowhere but to frustration and resignation to the hopelessness of his situation.

While current claims by government and departmental officials suggest that much is being done for our Veterans, we question the legitimacy of these claims because so far this year, some 56 Veterans have been driven to suicide. Jesse had been a highly skilled front line soldier who had experienced severe trauma during his service in Afghanistan in 2009/2010. For our son to receive such appalling deadly treatment at the hands of a government department charged with the duty of providing him with care and support is inexcusable. Common sense should dictate that current departmental leadership and their policies have driven the DVA to this low ebb and are not capable of overseeing the necessary total overhaul which is undoubtedly required.

Yours sincerely
Karen, John, Brendan and Kate Bird

AAO Administrative Arrangements Order **AAT** Administrative Ap
Force **ADFRP** Australian Defence Force Rehabilitation Program **AD**
Australian Institute of Health and Welfare **ANAO** Australian Natior
Training and Development Program **ATO** Australian Taxation Office **A**
therapy **CCS** Coordinated Client Support **CDC** consumer directed car
Chief of the Defence Force **CFTS** continuous full-time service **CI** con
Governments **COIN** counter-insurgency **CSC** Commonwealth Sup
Coordinated Veterans' Care xiv A BETTER WAY TO SUPPORT VETE
Defence Community Organisation **DFISA** Defence Force Income Su
Department of Human Services **DIPP** Defence Injury Prevention Pr
Rehabilitation and Compensation (Defence-related Claims) Act 198
Safety Committee **EDA** Extreme Disablement Adjustment **ESO** Ex-se
time equivalent **GARP** Guide to the Assessment of Rates of Veteran:
General practitioner **GST** Goods and Services Tax **HCH** Health Care I
Income Support Supplement **JHC** Joint Health Command **JTC** Joint
Service **MCRA** Military Rehabilitation and Compensation Act 2004 **M**
MRCA Military Rehabilitation and Compensation Act 2004 **MRCAE**
DRAFT REPORT xv and Training Scheme **MRCC** Military Rehabilitati
NMHC National Mental Health Commission **NZVAB** New Zealand V
for Economic Co-operation and Development **OHS** Occupational Hea
Productivity Commission **PCBU** persons conducting a business or unc
PI permanent impairment **PTSD** post-traumatic stress disorder **QA** qu
RMA Repatriation Medical Authority **RPBS** Repatriation Pharmace
Services League **RTW** return to work **SAM** Single Access Mechani
Statement of Principle **SRCA** Safety, Rehabilitation and Compens:
SRDP Special Rate of Disability Pension **TAC** Transport Accident Co
SUPPORT VETERANS DRAFT REPORT **TTTP** time taken to process
Centric Reform **VEA** Veterans' Entitlements Act 1986 **Veterans' M**.
Veterans' Home Care **VSC** Veteran Services Commission **VVCS** Vet
Rehabilitation Scheme **WH&S** Work Health and Safety **WHO** World

unal **ABS** Australian Bureau of Statistics **ADF** Australian Defence
ive dispute resolution **AGA** Australian Government Actuary **AIHW**
)ffice **APSC** Australian Public Service Commission **ATDP** Advocacy
:alian War Memorial **BoT** Board of Taxation **CBT** Cognitive behaviour
)mpensation for Detriment caused by Defective Administration **CDF**
:erval **CMA** contracted medical advisor **COAG** Council of Australian
)n Corporation **CTAS** Career Transition Assistance Scheme **CVC**
AFT REPORT **CWGC** Commonwealth War Graves Commission **DCO**
•wance **DFRDB** Defence Force Retirement and Death Benefits **DHS**
•**M&C** Department of the Prime Minister and Cabinet **DRCA** Safety,
:partment of Veterans' Affairs **DWHSC** Defence Work, Health and
misation **ESORT** ESO Round Table **FTB** Family Tax Benefit **FTE** full-
; **GARP-M** Guide to Determining Impairment and Compensation **GP**
` Information and communications technology **IL** initial liability **ISS**
a Command **MATES** Medicines Advice and Therapeutics Education
dle East Area of Operations **MEC** Medical Employment Classification
/ Rehabilitation and Compensation Act Education ABBREVIATIONS
mpensation Commission **NDIS** National Disability Insurance Scheme
dvisory Board **OBAS** On Base Advisory Service **OECD** Organisation
ifety **PAYG** pay-as-you-go **PBS** Pharmaceutical Benefits Scheme **PC**
PGPA Public Governance, Performance and Accountability Act 2013
rance **RAAF** Royal Australian Air Force **RC** Repatriation Commission
1efits Scheme **RPL** recognition of prior learning **RSL** Returned and
AT service category **SMRC** Specialist Medical Review Council **SoP**
1988 **SRCC** Safety, Rehabilitation and Compensation Commission
TPI Totally and Permanently Incapacitated xvi A BETTER WAY TO
d Nations **VCES** Veterans' Children Education Scheme **VCR** Veteran
:rans' Medicines Advice and Therapeutics Education Services **VHC**
Veterans Families Counselling Service **VVRS** Veterans' Vocational
ganization **WPIT** Welfare Payment Infrastructure Transformation.[14]

Not birds, but crocodiles

I sat down wanting to write about birds this morning but ended up going to the doctors instead, to get a referral under the mental health plan. Thinking about Dad and reading about veteran suicides had anger and sadness collecting like dust in the corners of me.

I was waiting at the doctors, reading about celebrity marriage break-ups, when my old neighbour Alan hobbled in and sat down by my side, not realising it was me.

When we were neighbours, Alan decided that the eucalypt at the front of my house needed trimming, because it was getting close to the telegraph wires. He turned up at my front door one morning, wearing only stubbies and thongs and holding a ladder.

'I'm going to trim your tree,' he told me.

'Oh, you don't need to,' I said, as I followed him to the tree and started holding the ladder. He obviously wasn't asking permission. As he leant the ladder on the branch he was about to saw, I tried again. 'You don't really need to, Alan. Be careful. Are you sure this is a good idea?'

I looked up at him on the ladder and realised he was wearing nothing under his faded stubbies. Despite his age, his state of undress and his dubious skills, he was a force I couldn't reckon with. I could only stand at the foot of the ladder, hoping not to be the thing that broke his fall when the branch broke or he was electrocuted. When he was satisfied, Alan took his ladder and went home, leaving my front porch covered in leaves and branches.

In the waiting room, I tapped him on the shoulder and said, 'Fancy meeting you here.' He commented on the increasing likelihood of meeting at the doctors as one aged, then started to tell me about his wedding.

'I got married, you know.'

'Really? Why?'

'To make sure my sister can't get anything when I'm gone.'

'How long have you and Mario been together?'

'Forty years.'

Alan was an aging and dissolute Hungarian with a home-style haircut, Mario a handsome and emotional Argentinian with soft brown eyes and a talent for sewing. They loved opera and German shepherds and gardening. Their dogs were always called Macho. When their first Macho died, they got a Macho #2 and so on. Macho #3 had such bad arthritis they needed to tend him night and day. They grew pennywort in their front garden to put in his food twice a day. Then, each morning and evening, they lugged him around the neighbourhood for a walk in a homemade sling.

Despite not admitting to any romance about the wedding, Alan proceeded to tell me all about it. It was in a registry office. He was worried that the person conducting the ceremony would be judgemental about him and Mario, but it had been a woman and she'd been lovely. They'd had a few neighbours as guests. Mario, he said, 'leaked' a few times. It took me a moment to work out he meant Mario had cried.

'She asked if we wanted rings and I said "no", but then I pulled out a ring from my pocket for Mario. A little gold band with five little diamonds. One for each letter of his name. And then he leaked again.'

'You old romantic. Didn't he know you were going to do that?'

'No, and then he started leaking.' Alan then went on to tell me about the reception, which they had at their house. Alan cooked crocodile stew.

'Crocodile stew? Why?'

'It's delicious.'

'Where would you even buy crocodile?'

'Marrickville, next door to Banana Joe's. It's frozen. It's expensive, about $20 a kilo.' He then went on to describe the whole process of cooking it so it tastes OK. At which point I zoned out.

'You lost me at crocodile I'm afraid, Alan.'

'But it's delicious,' he said, before continuing his monologue about the ideal times and temperatures for crocodile cooking.

I was worried that when my doctor saw me smiling at Alan, she would think I wasn't depressed enough to warrant a referral. I didn't even feel like I could muster the tears to convince her otherwise.

A *What the Fuck* look

One Sunday, my partner Adam and I visit his friend Gay at home. She's fighting cancer. (Why do you always have to say 'fighting cancer' and not 'coping with' or 'moving through'?) She's going through rounds of chemo and various operations and I sense, during our visit, that she doesn't necessarily want to talk about all her procedures, so I tell her about the birds that have set up home outside Adam's bedroom window.

We'd been watching a Currawong family nest for weeks; from the very first day the mother bird started setting a few sticks together on a fork in the tree and pressing them into place with her breast. (It must be so frustrating not having hands.) Over the next week or so, the nest took shape and then, one day, the mother took up residence in it almost full time. We figured she must have laid her eggs.

Adam was pretty down at that point, tired and stressed, and reading about trauma all the time for his work as a psychologist had taken its toll. He saw the nest as depressing. Something was bound to go wrong. It was bound to fall out of the tree or cuckoos would come and kill the chicks or the eggs just wouldn't hatch. Despite his fears, days passed and everyone survived. We watched as the dad bird brought worms to the mum and popped them in her mouth or they'd both fly off to find food. Most often though, she sat, and he fed her.

We became a bit bird obsessed, googling things about them while lying in bed and talking about them when we were out.

'Do birds have knees?'

'Why don't birds fly everywhere? Why do they walk sometimes? I'd fly everywhere if I was a bird.'

'They look so funny when they walk.' We stood laughing at a flat-footed seagull walking about on the ground.

'You can fly, you know?' I told it as it ran past us on red clown feet.

'How long does it take for eggs to hatch?'

Adam had been reading about them, about how birds can lay eggs over time and how only once they are all laid will they fertilise them. We talked about chicken eggs.

'They are basically chicken periods,' he said.

'Oh God. I don't know if I'll ever be able to eat them again.'

We watched, days later, as tiny bald baked-bean heads – all beak and bulging blind eyes – popped up over the edge of the nest when the parents went to get worms. We worried when it got windy or rainy. I'd text Adam to ask how the babies were. We watched the hungriest baby on the right grow biggest and fastest. We saw the mother bird sit higher and higher in the nest until she skirted the top of it, her three big babies squashed underneath. One morning, Adam's cat Bowser snuck into the room and got up on the bed. The mother bird noticed and, once I'd shooed him out and shut the door, she landed on the balcony wall and gave me what I understood as a *What the Fuck?* look.

We noticed their strange little bird rituals and wondered, in turn, if they noticed our human ones. We imagined them watching us having sex and saying to each other, 'What do you think they are doing?'

After finishing my bird rave, Gay told us about her neighbours, one of whom was a doctor. They found an ibis with a broken wing and the doctor operated on it, to fix it. When the neighbours were about to go on holiday, they didn't know what to do with the bird, so they took it with them. The two of them and an ibis with a sling, off to the coast.

A 'What The Fuck?' look.

Podría morir pronto

Mum lost two men she loved to war. Her brother Len went to fight in WWII and never came home. She only saw him one more time, on an ill-fated holiday with Denise and me, many years after. To be honest, I didn't really mean to invite my mum on that holiday. It was my big 'coming of age' trip after university. I was in Barcelona with my friends. We had scored some black hash in a dodgy back street, taken it to the sea baths and eaten it crumbled over ice cream. For some reason, I decided then was a good time to go to the post office and book a call to Mum in Australia.

My friends stared at me, breathing through their mouths, slightly wasted, as I set off by myself to the post office to make my call. I was fine getting there and booking the call but as I waited, I started to feel really faint, like I'd pass out at any minute. I started running through the few Spanish words I knew, to see if I could cobble together anything to say if things got worse. I didn't know the word for faint. All I could come up with was, 'Podría morir pronto – I might die soon.' Then they called my name.

I don't remember much about the call. All I remember is the wave of guilt and regret (or was it regret and guilt) that engulfed me when I hung up. 'You should come meet me and Denise. It will be fun. Go on,' I must have said. 'OK, I will,' she must have agreed.

So that's how I found myself sitting beside Denise at Heathrow waiting for Mum's plane to manoeuvre itself on the tarmac. Denise was chewing her nails. I slapped her hand away from her mouth. 'Don't do that.' We'd stayed up late the night before, talking. Denise had told me she'd chosen to go to uni in Canberra to get away from Mum and live her own life, like it was some kind of confession. It had been a year since I'd seen Mum and two since Denise had. When she walked out from the barriers with her dizzy step, with legs seeming to be at cross-purposes, my first thought was that her sunglasses were too big for her head.

Despite all our assurances that we'd find somewhere nice to stay, Mum had booked a B&B before she left Australia and had sent a non-refundable deposit by cheque. It was so Mum to say, 'OK,' then do what she wanted to anyway. To no-one's surprise (not ours, anyway) the place was an hour's drive out of central London on a dingy suburban street. A tired-looking woman in curlers and a dressing gown, smoking a cigarette, opened the door to us. She eyed each of us in turn, then opened the door a bit more to reveal a man aged about thirty standing behind her. She stood aside to let us in but didn't turn her back on us.

'This is my son Terry this is the dining room breakfast is at eight please follow me.'

On the way up the stairs, she pointed out the bathroom we shared with her permanent guests before we reached our room. 'This is your room,' she said, as she pulled out a big wad of keys, unlocked the door and pushed it open with a flourish. Inside the room, where thick grey carpet had seemingly grown over the floor and heavy curtains smothered the light from outside, sat a sad old double bed cowering under chenille.

I tried to be polite, tried not to state the obvious.

'There's three of us. We'll need another bed.'

The woman insisted she was only expecting two.

'Look, this is stupid,' I said. 'Give us another bed or give us our money back.'

She insisted the money was strictly NON-REFUNDABLE then spun on her heel and stormed down the hall, came back with a camp bed and a couple of blankets, left them in the corner of the room, then left the room, trailing her cigarette ash and her son behind her.

When one attends Eisteddfods and music auditions, the scene is set for the learning and budding musicians to be judged by a panel of adjudicators invariably consisting of established and experienced musicians within their field. Does one need to ask who knows more: the judges or the competitors? This seems an almost silly question but in in the flurry of excitement of claims that avian males are more beautiful, more accomplished, bigger and better overall, the researchers literally forgot to ask (over decades) how the females could judge unless they had some gifts and even special talents themselves.[15]

Gisela Kaplan — *Bird bonds*

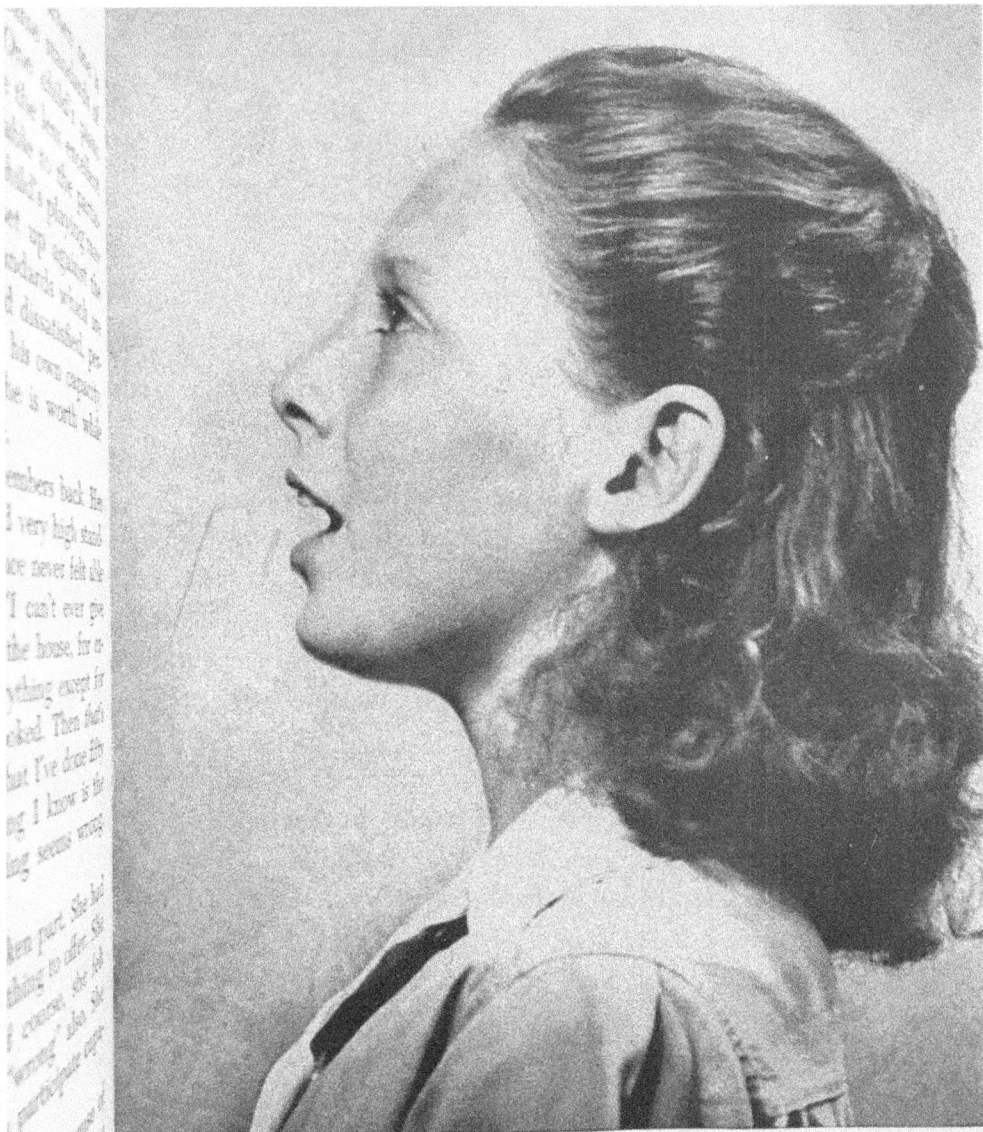

Photograph by A. Pierce Artran.

Singing is Jane's way of contributing to family life.

Visiting Uncle Len

Uncle Len died in WWII. On our first day in London, Mum wanted to visit his grave. We caught a bus to the cemetery and there, stretched before us, were rows and rows, as far we could see, of the same little gravestones. How would we ever find Uncle Len in there? Mum started to cry. I started crying too and we hadn't even found him yet. All those little blocks of stone, all those young lives summed up so brutally.

Denise found something like a street directory to look up your loved ones in and when we found Uncle Len's grave the crying got worse. Mum started again and I couldn't help but join in, even though I'd never met him. Then Denise started, dropping the directory on to the ground, pushing her fists into her eyes and heaving her shoulders, like a sad two-year-old. I was crying for the war and the holiday that was turning sour and for myself and for Mum and for Dad, who'd died eight years before, and then for Mum again, because she really loved him and then for Uncle Len.

Mum dropped to her knees and put the flowers she'd brought for Len on his grave. She told him how sad she was that he'd gone, how she missed him, how everyone did. She ran a hand over the top of his little gravestone, said goodbye, then stood up to go.

I tried to sleep in the camp bed that night, but it was too saggy and uncomfortable. Instead, I watched the sleeping lumps of their two bodies rise and fall. I had to drive the hire car. I should have been in the double bed. I shut my eyes, but my blank miserable stare just looked at the inside of my lids.

The next morning, we crept downstairs and were met by the woman, still in curlers and a dressing gown, still smoking. We joined the group already assembled in the dining room, three permanent guests who all had thick glasses and curly hair, which they'd all tried to slick down. The collars and cuffs of their shirts were dirty. Terry sat at the head of the table. We sat on one side of the table; the three men sat facing us, like a trick mirror. They worked as computer programmers down the road. The woman cooked and cleaned for them and they all had their own room. After what seemed like an age, our breakfast arrived and was whacked down in front of us. Scrambled eggs, toast and tea. The tea was weak, the toast cold.

Children of a Lesser God

Denise suggested she might go and see a movie called *Children of a Lesser God* while I drove Mum to Buckingham Palace. I complained about having to go to the Palace and Mum got upset. To keep the peace, we all ended up going to the Palace *and* the movie. But the peace was short-lived. Somehow, later that night, the events of the afternoon opened a floodgate of things unsaid for years, unleashing a tidal wave of honesty and guilt.

Children of a Lesser God is about 'a new speech teacher at a school for the deaf who falls in love with the janitor, a deaf woman speechless by choice'.

The tagline of the film is *Love has a language all of its own.*[16]

That night, back in our room after the movie, our love had a language all of its own.

Mum said, 'Don't worry, you'll be rid of me soon. As soon as we get back home you won't have to bother about me.'

She said, 'Thank God your father isn't here. I'm so ashamed. I never knew I was such a bad mother.'

She said, 'If I'd have known you felt like that, I would have killed myself. As soon as we're back you won't have to see me again. I'll just leave you alone.'

Lollies and landscapes

We left the next day. The woman and Terry watched as we filed past and went to find a nicer place to stay in the centre of London. We resolved to try harder with each other, to start again.

After the argument, Mum was quieter than usual, lost in her thoughts. She tagged along behind Denise and me, and mimed sightseeing. If you asked whether she was having a good time, she'd say, 'Yes,' but it was as if you'd asked if London was the capital of England. She answered matter-of-factly, 'Yes.'

She looked out the car window, but I could tell she wasn't thinking about the landscape. I wished I knew what she was thinking. She saw me looking, smiled and offered me a lolly. Her back seat had become an expanse of lolly wrappers, old tissues, pillows and blankets. I didn't want a lolly, but she had one. She unwrapped it slowly and popped it into her mouth. She loved caramels. She was the type of woman who could make a caramel last an hour. She could savour things like lollies and landscapes that Denise and I devoured.

Mum's version (from her travel diary)

Sat: *Very wet. Potatoes 6p a pound. Had delicious scones and jam and cream at a quaint little place. Stayed the night at Holford. 21 pounds. Family downstairs had a verbal in the middle of the night.*
Good English Breakfast.

Sun: *Went to Wells. Saw St Andrews Cathedral. Beautiful.*

Fri: *Went into Lincoln and had a look at St Paul's Cathedral. Beautiful. Petrol 9 pounds 50. On to London (freezing cold).*
Found the B&B I'd booked from Australia. Left our bags then returned the car. Decided to go to the movies. Saw Children of a Lesser God. Quite Good. Caught underground train home. B&B a long walk from the station. Cold. Dark. Horrible. Fold up bed had been put up for the third bed. Not wide enough for a snake.
Breakfast, one choice, scrambled eggs. Didn't like the place.
Woman returned cheque and charged 40 pounds. We had messed her around a bit.

Family secrets (I know about) #3 – How Mary Killed Ivy

Mum had a habit of casually dropping heavy facts into a conversation (like how she tried to get rid of me with castor oil or how the colour of my shirt matched my father's corpse). She seemed unaware of the ripples they created. She dropped another when we were driving through Cardiff in our hire car, on her first visit there. She told us as if she'd just remembered, though it wasn't the sort of story you could forget.

From her back seat, Mum piped up about her mother's sister Mary and Mary's daughter Ivy who was born blind and deaf. They had lived in Cardiff. She said that Ivy used to scream and cry if she didn't get what she wanted. She ran Mary into the ground. She gave her hell and it went on for years, until Mary killed her. But she didn't kill Ivy because of her behaviour. Mary said the Devil made her do it. He came and chased her around the bed, held her down and told her to do it. And so, she killed her.

This was the first time I'd heard about Mary and Ivy. As I drove through the streets of Cardiff, I tried to imagine what it would have been like for them. Ivy would have trusted her mother completely. Mary would have cared for Ivy's body like it was her own. What must have been going through her head when she took her girl and killed her? How did she do it? Did she get a gun and shoot her while she slept or did she get a pillow and hold it over Ivy's head so she couldn't breathe? Did Ivy kick and struggle? What was she thinking about?

In silence #1

It's Friday and I'm in Melbourne visiting my daughter, Stella. While she's at work, I've been trying to write in the city library. I've been thinking about silence.

All sorts of people come to this library to read and study and eat (when did it became OK to eat in libraries?). I was here yesterday reading about an Australian journalist called Edward Honey, who first suggested honouring the war dead in silence. He served as a soldier in the British army in WWI and was medically discharged due to shellshock. After his discharge, he stayed on in London and worked as a journalist. Honey watched the wild celebrations of the Armistice in November 1918 and later felt compelled to write a letter to the *London Evening News* on 8 May 1919 (under the pseudonym Warren Foster), suggesting a solemn ceremony of:

> Five little minutes only. Five silent minutes of national remembrance. A very sacred intercession. Communion with the Glorious Dead who won us peace, and from the communion new strength, hope and faith in the morrow. Church services, too, if you will, but in the street, the home, the theatre, anywhere, indeed, where Englishmen and their women chance to be, surely in this five minutes of bitter-sweet silence there will be service enough.[17]

Though Honey was the first to suggest this form of remembrance, he wasn't the only one. In preparation for the first anniversary of the armistice, King George V invited Honey and others for a private rehearsal of a silent ceremony with the Grenadier Guards at Buckingham Palace. Even the guards had trouble standing still and quiet for five minutes during the rehearsal, so the king decided it was way too long. Days before the anniversary, he formally decreed the two minutes' silence.

> It is my desire and hope that at the hour when the Armistice came into force, the 11th hour of the 11th day of the 11th month, there may be for the brief space of two minutes a complete suspension of all our normal activities ... so that, in perfect stillness, the thoughts of everyone may concentrate on reverent remembrance of the Glorious Dead.[18]

It is one minute now. The last time I stopped to observe the silence was a year ago at Newtown Festival, though it wasn't much of a 'perfect stillness'. Most people didn't realise what was going on when a lone bugler started playing the Last Post at the foot of the stage. A small wave of quiet passed through the crowd. Some stood with heads bowed, knowing and respectful; some looked around confused; others frothed milk for lattes or chased children.

That bugle call carries a sadness now that it didn't before. Originally, the calls of an army bugler were used to help soldiers keep track of time.[19] Different 'songs' let them know if it was time to wake for the day, time to eat, time to work, or (with the Last Post) to let them know the day was over, the camp was secure, and it was time to sleep.

In silence #2

I was sitting in the library thinking about remembrance and silence, and I started to think about all the silences in my family. We remembered things in silence too, but those silences weren't about honour.

While I was in the middle of my reverie the woman a few desks down began:

unwrapping lollies wrapped in cellophane,

then twisted her Coke bottle until it sighed,

AHHH,

before she upended it,

and slugged it back,

Glug, Glug, Glug ... AHHH,

then rearranged her notebook,

and purple backpack,

and phone holder,

and computer,

and pens (clicking them a few times for good measure),

typed a few words (how can you type so loudly?),

then had more lollies,

and some chips (CHIPS!?).

Why is no one else looking?

This is a library.

She's not talking,

but she's not silent.

Then I noticed her pièce de résistance. In the USB socket of the power point in front of her, she'd installed a small personal fan. It was in the shape of WWI biplane and was being flown by a pink kitten wearing pink goggles. I could just hear the hum of her little pink plane over the sounds of her silence.

Family secrets (that I know about) #4

In her kitchen in Canberra,
Mum's sister Ivy,
pulled Denise aside,
and whispered in her ear,
'It was syphilis, you know.
That's what made Mary do it.'

Heart story #3 (shortest version)

I was going to put a love story in here. Well, it wasn't really a love story. It was about how I *thought* I fell in love with someone. It was already in two parts and I hadn't even finished (I was going into great detail), but I've changed my mind. I'm going to give you the bare bones of it instead.

So, the gist of it is that a guy I knew just a little, who was well connected in the international art scene, came to visit me at my gallery in Sydney and started having what later turned out to be a heart attack in our storeroom. At first it was only something that felt like a pulled muscle or a pinched nerve.

'My neck is killing me,' he said. 'I must have pulled a muscle.'

When I drove him and his friends across town to another gallery, he broke out in a sweat and needed to wind the window down. 'Aren't you guys hot? It's boiling in here,' he said.

After I left them, his pain got worse. By the end of the night, he was in the emergency department of a nearby hospital. Death brushed past him on his way in. He texted me the next day:

I'm in St Vincents. I've had a heart attack.

The reason I'm telling you about this 'love affair' at all is because this guy looked a bit like my dad and was about the same age as my dad when he died of a heart attack and I had two simultaneous responses to the situation:

1. After his heart attack, I fell madly in love with this guy (I thought) and was compelled to be by his side, to comfort him, to talk with him. I looked at his hands lying on the sheets and

longed to hold them. I would have crawled into the hospital bed beside him. I would have married him.

2. I knew that whatever I was feeling was about my dad. Each night after I visited the guy in hospital, I'd wait until my daughter, Stella, had fallen asleep and I would sob deeply and painfully into my pillow, which I used to muffle the sound of my crying. When I visited him one day, he said, 'I thought about your dad last night,' and I burst into tears again. The nurse entering the room spun on her heel, apologising for interrupting. I wanted to say, 'It's OK. It's not about him.' Once, I was speaking to the guy when my father's face flashed onto his. I knew what was going on. I had a voice in my head telling me, 'You know this is about your dad, right?' but I felt powerless to react otherwise.

There's probably other stuff I could tell you, like how he was full of hot air, how his talk was much bigger than his reality. How he'd text me whenever the mood struck him (i.e. 4am my time) about whatever was on his mind. How he said, 'If I'd been stranded here any longer, I would have ended up marrying you.' How he paid to fly me to Japan to meet him for four days because he simply couldn't wait until I'd be in Europe a few months later.

I didn't shit the whole time I was in Japan but couldn't tell him about it because I didn't really know him. I knew him enough, though, to know that he wouldn't laugh.

My inability to shit didn't stop me from eating as many oysters and as much sushi, and drinking as much sake as possible. He was paying. He made sure I remembered. After one particularly extravagant meal, when we got out to the street, he pulled out the receipt and let me know exactly how much it cost. By day three I felt like a science experiment, but I continued eating and drinking, nevertheless. I figured something had to give, eventually.

I had given him a copy of *Portnoy's Complaint* by Philip Roth and, even though he said he'd read it, I knew he hadn't, particularly when, after another fruitless trip to the toilet I commented, 'I feel like Portnoy's father.' (Chronically constipated, Portnoy's father said he wanted to 'dig it out with a spoon'.)

He didn't understand.

The short end to this story is, he got home, and he got back with his ex, but he also kept calling and texting me, telling me he loved me. The last time I saw him, after promising to take me for a drink, he turned up to my stand at an art fair, on the last day of the fair, with a plastic champagne flute half-filled with warm champagne and a colleague of some sort. He proceeded to brag about taking his best clients out for an expensive meal.

He was nothing like my dad.

Funny how you can absorb lots of insults and slights and disappointments from someone and then they do something that can seem pretty banal, but it's the one thing that finally does it for you. Well, when I say you, I mean me. That's the way I get angry. Very slowly, then very decisively, then I'm done.

1. Face, do not run away.
2. Accept, do not fight.
3. Float past, do not arrest and listen-in.
4. Let time pass, do not be impatient with time.[20]

Dr Claire Weekes — *Peace from Nervous Suffering*

Boredom can lead to excess

In her claim for a War Widow's pension, Mum wrote:

> I had known my late husband John Renfrew Rennex eighteen
> months before he joined the Army. Twelve months after his
> joining up we were married, during this period he enjoyed good
> health and smoked only an occasional cigarette. Throughout the
> following twelve years he was a loving husband and good father
> to our three daughters, we enjoyed a happy family life, he both
> smoked and drank only in moderation.
>
> In June 1965 he was sent to Vietnam, on his return the stress
> he had been under during service there, resulted in him smoking
> very heavily and this continued until his death.

In the internal discussions regarding her claim, the medical officer of
the Repatriation Board dismissed Dad's early death being related to
his war service.

> The veteran's wife claims that the stress of service in VietNam
> caused the veteran to increase his smoking … He may well have
> increased his intake during his VietNam service, but this may not
> have been because of stress. In a man already entrenched in the
> habit, boredom can lead to excess, and there is no indication in
> the service documents of any unusual stress, or any psychiatric
> disturbance resulting therefrom.

He was just a fat and bored smoker who had trouble adjusting to
civilian life.

Similarly, the veteran had a 'weight problem'... He had been grossly obese for a number of years after the eligible period, again despite medical advice. His widow claims a change in her late husband's personality after he returned from VietNam. The symptoms she describes, however, could have resulted from the change involved in leaving the service and adjusting to civilian life. There is nothing in the file to link these with the veteran's service.[21]

That would have been it for Mum's claim if it hadn't been for other widows like Mrs McGlynn. She took her rejected claim for a pension to the Federal Court and won. Her husband had been a prisoner of the Japanese between 1942 and 1945, where he became an avid smoker. He died of lung cancer in 1976.

In the case of *McGlynn v Repatriation Commission – Entitlement to pension upon death*[22] – the judge found there had been an error in the original determination by the Repatriation Board. Mrs McGlynn's claim was originally rejected because she couldn't prove her husband's death was caused by his war service. But, back then, a pension couldn't be refused unless it was proved beyond reasonable doubt that his death *wasn't* related to war service – a subtle yet huge difference.

Mum's eligibility for a pension rested on smoke.

That was a cigarette in the dog's mouth.

A visit

I was staying with Mum.
I was helping her while she was being treated for cancer.
I woke up in the middle of the night unable to breathe.
I found Dad sitting on my bed.
He was patting me on the shoulder, trying to comfort me.
He'd accidentally sat on my chest instead of the bed and didn't realise.
I couldn't breathe or speak, so I couldn't tell him.
I had to wait for him to notice.
Then he disappeared.

That was a good memory. The only fucking one. That beautiful bird just going about its business with all that crazy stuff going on. Whole flocks of them would fly over – Once a grenade hit close to some trees and there were these birds taking off like quail, ever' which way. We thought it was snowing up instead of down.[23]

Bobby Ann Mason – *In Country*

Life as a bird

After weeks of avoiding it, I drove out to Mum's place at North Ryde, opened the garage roller door and stood looking at all the stuff we needed to deal with now that she'd died. Boxes and boxes of crap.

Mum had managed to filter out the precious stuff of life and keep the chaff. I knew I'd find crystal dust catchers, toy clowns and novelty spoons but not the old 'kimono' Dad had brought back from Vietnam or the letters she'd burned. She'd thrown out the bags of clothes I'd left there for safekeeping too. Well, she never actually admitted to throwing those out.

Before I'd left on an adventure overseas, I had collected all my favourite op-shop treasures – a silver lamé bolero, leather pants, a black lace shirt – and stored them in bags in the garage at North Ryde. When I returned a year later, after living out of a backpack and wearing the same few clothes day after day, I was looking forward to retrieving them. I looked everywhere for them – in the garage, in the linen closet, in my old wardrobe. Nothing. They were gone. I asked Mum if she knew where they were.

'No,' she said, 'I don't remember any bags.'

'Don't you remember?' I asked. 'I left them here. They were in plastic garbage bags. I left them in the garage.'

'Hmmm, maybe they were thrown out by mistake … I mean … if they were in garbage bags …'

I asked Maree.

'No,' she said, 'I didn't see any bags.'

It was my first day back in Australia in over a year. I sat watching TV at Mum's house, fuming.

Maree only came clean after Mum died.

'Yeah, she threw them out. She told me not to tell you.'

'Bitch,' I said. 'I knew she was lying. I can't believe she wouldn't admit to it. You're a bitch too. You should have told me and saved me all that time looking for them.'

Maree shrugged and smiled. 'She threw my record collection out too,' she said.

Now I was standing at the house in North Ryde looking into the garage when I heard a heavy animal noise, a thud and some scratching coming from the back. Whatever made it was bigger than an insect, judging from the noise. A cat? A rat? I thought about throwing something towards the noise but couldn't find anything to throw, so I just waited.

A dusty Myna bird emerged from between the cardboard boxes and staggered about a bit. Who knows how long it had been there. The garage hadn't been opened for at least a week. It didn't look like it would be able to muster the strength to fly. Should I get it water? It looked pretty dehydrated. I stood at the entrance to the garage and panicked. The bird stood still too, looking at me looking at it, then it stumbled around some more. I then did what Mum and I would always do in situations where we didn't know what to do. I went to get Mr Mullens.

He came over and we stood looking at the bird as it careered around a bit more. Then, just like that it ran past us, goose-stepping out of the garage, before falling into some bushes along the path.

'That was easy,' he said. 'Should I mow the lawns for you while I'm here?'

A white Christmas

The first Christmas after Mum dies is, as I expect, horrible.

Maree invites me for lunch at the Rum Runner restaurant at Birkenhead Point with her partner Peter, their daughter Elena, Peter's father Hector, and Hector's girlfriend Esme. I arrive earlier than them and go inside. The tables are all empty and the Rum Runner smells of old cooking oil. I walk outside again and wait out the front.

Peter's red car pulls up. Maree is on the phone to the people at the restaurant. Hector is old and sick and so bent over now, he can hardly move. They need to work out how to get him inside. There are two ways to get to the restaurant; one is up a lot of stairs, the other along a long ramp. I suggest to Peter that he should park in the parking station and use the ramp so his father doesn't have to negotiate the steps. Peter jumps back in the car and drives off. I go and wait near the ramp. I look up. Peter is on the third level of the car park.

'Is this where you meant?' he yells.

'No,' I yell back, 'I meant ground level.'

He disappears and reappears seconds later near the ramp on ground level, then begins the process of negotiating with Hector's broken old body. There isn't much affection going to waste between them.

'No, no,' Peter says, 'lean on me, I said. Bring your right foot all the way up to the gutter ... further ... right up I said. Now lift the other one. That's right. Lean on me.'

Maree unloads Elena and her paraphernalia. Both of them are wearing wrap-around reflector sunglasses. As Elena is only four months old, hers are held on with elastic.

We go in. Five tables of half-hearted revellers are strewn throughout the large space and the air-conditioning is on high, so the restaurant is too cold and too quiet. The buffet is full of pre-carved meats stacked under warm lights. Tinsel festoons any surface it can, like a psychotic vine, and there's a piano, but no player. We take our seats. Hector is so bent over when he is sitting at the table that his face almost touches his plate.

Maree asks me to hold Elena while she organises various baby accessories. I'm not that experienced with babies. I sit her on my lap, facing me, and we regard each other. She is something of a beacon for me. A month after watching my mother take her last breath, I was there waiting for Elena to take her first, taking photos. She had to be dragged into the world, with forceps and suction and brute strength. When her head came out, it was bright blue. And as she paused, head out, body in, between contractions, I took photos. All I could say was, 'Oh My God,' then click and wind, 'Oh My God.' I only had black and white film. No one had warned me about the colours.

There's no need to order food. It's all there in the buffet. We order wine and the waiter puts it in an ice bucket behind my chair. Before the bottle is even half-finished, the person at the next table knocks it over on the way to the buffet and says, 'It was a stupid place to put it anyway.'

The piano player arrives.

Hector has not said a word since we arrived, except to ask for food or drink. He is up to his cup of tea and dessert while we are still eating our entrées. Maree and Peter hardly speak to each other. They direct their attention to Elena who, like Hector, is already on her dessert. I consume a little bit of bread and turkey and half a glass of wine. Maree and I speak about letting out Mum's house. Peter insists that if we do, it is almost inevitable that someone will put their fist through a wall. Maree tells me she has trouble mowing the lawns. I hadn't even thought about the lawns.

'I'll do them,' I say.

Those fucking lawns again.

The bill comes. It's $45 a head plus $2.50 for the warm filter coffee and more for the wine that was spilt. The piano player is singing *I'm dreaming of a white Christmas. Just like the ones I used to know* and I think I am going to cry. I get up and go to the toilet. In the cubicle my bottom lip drops. The tears that have been waiting patiently all day start leaking down my cheeks. I can still hear the piano player singing *May your days be merry and bright. And may all your Christmases be white*, while I stand facing the toilet, willing myself together, just until I get out of the Rum Runner.

I return to the table, pay $50 and leave to drive up to Whale Beach, to my friend Andy's house. He has a real family Christmas. With brothers and sisters and mothers and fathers and kids and leftovers and digesting and talking and laughter. That night Andy and I drive to meet our friends at Nielsen Park. We swim in the dark harbour until late at night, holding on to the shark net and watching the lights of the city nearby.

Acceptance with understanding dulls the edge of terror.[24]

Dr Claire Weekes — *Peace from Nervous Suffering*

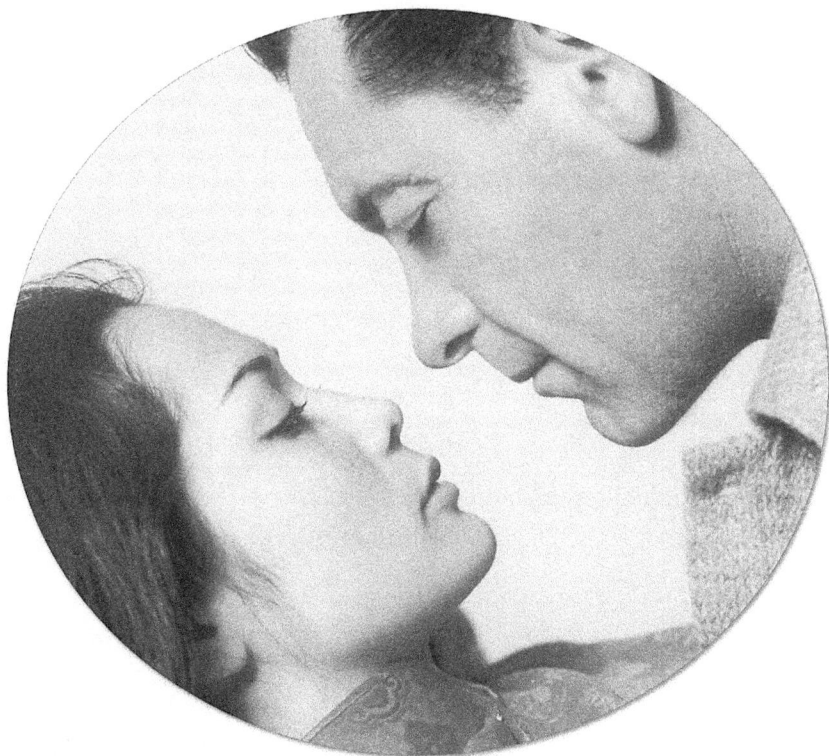

Someone brings two fingers up to their lips,
It looks like they are saying,
Shhhh ... be quiet.

When they exhale,
the unspoken words
are expressed as smoke.

When I see someone smoking,
I wonder what it is they aren't able to say.

I have termed it a 'whimpering' call and it is the closest to crying in an animal that I have yet heard ... and may be emitted at the time when a small nestling tawny frogmouth has lost its parents and, at another time, when the juvenile tawny frogmouth is about to leave the territory ... the frogmouth tends to sit still through the night without feeding and the only sound it makes are these haunting, quiet, whimpering cries ... The only other context in which I have heard this call is after the resident female had lost her partner in a road accident. She 'cried' for days and I wonder, in this strong pair bond, whether or not her rejection of a gallery of suitors for two years running post-partner death was related to the strength of her bond to her dead partner. [25]

Gisela Kaplan – Tawny Frogmouth

Death as a bird

I heard a story not that long ago on a podcast called *This American Life*. It was by Kathie Russo, the wife of Spalding Gray, a writer and actor best known for his monologue *Swimming to Cambodia*, based on his experiences working on the film *The Killing Fields* and about the troubles in Cambodia. On 10 January 2004, Spalding went missing.

> Witnesses said they saw him on the Staten Island Ferry that night. Two months later, his body was pulled out of the East River. Kathie tells the story of the night he disappeared, and about how, in the weeks following, she and each of their three children were visited by a bird, who seemed to be delivering a message to them.[26]

For three days in a row, a bird came into their house and flew around. She knew from Irish folklore that if you find a bird alive in your house, it's the spirit of a recently deceased loved one, who is at peace. If you find a dead bird, their spirit is restless. She knew the bird was Spalding, so on the third day she said to it, 'We're OK, you can go now, Spalding.'

It never returned after that.

I thought of North Ryde when I heard her story. My bird had been in the garage. Even though it was Mum who'd recently died, the garage was Dad's domain. Perhaps his spirit had hung around the tool shelves long enough to look after her.

I'm glad we found him before he died and set him free.

Frankly thanks

I visited Vietnam once. When Stella was six years old. I remember because I learnt how to say 'she is six years old' in Vietnamese, *cô ấy sáu tuổi*. It wasn't a pilgrimage to find out about my dad, more an attempt to save my failing relationship with Stella's father, Dave.

I spent the whole two weeks in Vietnam holding Stella's hand. It was a new way of travelling for me, being constantly attached to someone. She hated Vietnam at first and begged to go home. The sights, sounds and smells were too much for her – clusters of dead ducks hanging by their legs, squealing pigs in bamboo sleeves hanging off the sides of bikes, bits of animal bodies displayed on tables in the morning market. She was such a beautiful, pale, blue-eyed child people would often stare or point at her, come up to hug her, take her photo or pinch her cheeks.

In Hanoi we lined up with thousands of locals on New Year's Day to visit Chairman Ho's body in the Mausoleum. We waited hours to shuffle past his strangely yellowed corpse, sandwiched between people in tears. In Hoi An we got personalised pink satin sandals made. In Sapa we got our hair plaited by young local girls. In Ho Chi Minh City we visited both the water park and the War Remnants Museum (originally called Exhibition House for US Puppet Crimes in 1975, then re-named Exhibition House for Crimes of War and Aggression in 1990 – before the warming of relations with the US led to it being called The War Remnants Museum from 1995).[27]

Dave and I took it in turns to go inside the museum. One of us would wait out the front with Stella, watching her climb over rusting military relics – downed fighter jets and armoured tanks – while the other would go inside to look at the displays. They pulled no punches in their displays – deformed foetuses in jars of formaldehyde, grisly photos of mutilation and disused guillotines showing what had been done in the name of war.

At the entrance to the museum there was a donation box that had the words FRANKLY THANKS written either side of a coin slot.

One of Dad's photos from Vietnam

Different angles

At the start of this project, I did a writing course with a group of other writers, all women. One of them happened to be from Vietnam. She was writing about her family and their journey to Australia. They had fled Vietnam as refugees in the 1970s and had ended up living in North Ryde. I didn't quite know how or whether I should alter the way I presented my work, to protect her feelings. She seemed pretty fragile and spoke often of her struggles with depression and self-doubt – struggles I was familiar with myself. I probed her gently about whether it was too painful for her to hear my stories. She said it was OK. I hoped it was. I felt, ultimately, that we were both writing about the same thing, the devastation of war, from different angles.

If you can think about something like birds, you can get outside of yourself, and it doesn't hurt as much. That's the whole idea. That's the whole challenge for the human race.[28]

Bobby Ann Mason – *In Country*

Another visit to the War Memorial

On another visit to the War Memorial, one of the librarians in the Research Centre suggests I look for information about my dad in the official histories. I thank her for her help but decide I don't really want official stories, so I poke around in the catalogue of the archive instead. I concentrate on the records that aren't already available online, fill out a little form for each file I want to request (taking a stab at what their contents might be) insert it into a clock to be date- and time-stamped in triplicate, then place the stamped form in a little wooden box and wait for the files to be retrieved.

I go grab a coffee while I wait, passing through the Hall of Valour and the Aircraft Hall, walking towards Anzac Hall then turning right to get to the Landing Place café. There's red poppies on everything here – on staff uniforms, signage, and all through the gift shop, where you can stock up on poppy mugs, pins, aprons, tea towels, trays, umbrellas, purses and even a poppy draught excluder.

The café overlooks Anzac Hall – a vast space filled with various large aircrafts and pieces of equipment. I had just read, before this visit, that the planned $500 million renovation and extension to the War Memorial will increase Anzac Hall threefold, and that Tony Abbott is being mooted as a replacement board member now that he's been voted out of parliament.

(Abbott was appointed in 2019. In 2020, family history volunteers at the Memorial were warned by management that if they commented on the planned extension publicly, or even liked someone's Facebook comment, they were in danger of losing their volunteer role at the Memorial.[29])

On the way back to the research room I detour past a Roll of Honour that:

> records and commemorates members of the Australian armed forces who have died during or as a result of war service, or for Post-1945 conflicts, warlike service, non-warlike service and certain peacetime operations.[30]

Dad's name isn't on it. He needed to have died between 3 August 1962 and 29 April 1975 to be included.

I wander back sullenly to the research room, shitty on my dad's behalf, put my bag in a locker, grab a sharpened pencil and notebook (no pens allowed) and go through the folders I've requested, one at a time, as per the procedures.

I find comments from women whose sons or partners returned changed or didn't return at all. In her *'Brief account ... relating to the death of her son in South Vietnam'*, Mrs Sylvia Bink wrote:

> *The worst part for me was that my son would kill someone he didn't know.*
> *That was war.*[31]

I find a folder of love letters from Sgt WF Hacking to Kathy, his fiancée at the time.[32] He was the first Australian soldier killed in South Vietnam and she believed he was killed by an ally. As well as his letters, there are news clippings about his death and interviews with her. His letters were written on different types of paper, dashed off in between assignments, occasionally typed so they were more legible, though in those cases half of the letter was about the difficulty of typing.

On 11 October 1962 he wrote:

> *My dearest, sweetest darling,*
> *I'm just about at the end of a not very satisfactory week, and*
> *thank goodness, a perfect bastard of a week (excuse my French)*
> *everything wrong. Not a thing right, and to top it off I'm down to*
> *my last few pages of writing paper...*

On 31 May 1963 he wrote his last letter. He lived only a few more hours after it was written.

> *This comes to you from a mountain top in the middle of the very*
> *deep jungle. Have been here for a few days now, and am taking*
> *this opportunity of a re-supply to get this little letter away to you.*
> *From where I look across to where we will be moving to, it is not*
> *a very encouraging sight, and when I look back to where we came*
> *from, to here, I find it very hard to believe that I actually did walk*
> *it. My bum was nearly dragging. I have found quite a few things*
> *about my physical condition which don't please me overmuch.*
> *My appetite for operations will have been whetted by the time*
> *this little jaunt is over ...*

In another file I find photocopied newspaper clippings about the first soldiers sent home from Vietnam in 1966.[33] One shows a photo of a young man lying under a sheet with a bandaged head, looking at the camera with his one eye not covered by fabric. The caption reads:

Private Boris Ornowski, 22, of Fairfield, Sydney, seriously ill with head and body injuries from an accidental grenade blast at Bien Hoa, is gently lifted from a plane at Sydney. 'I cannot say what is in my heart – it is too bitter,' said his weeping Polish mother as he was taken to Concord Repatriation Hospital. Private Ornowski was born in captivity in Germany.

Another clipping shows the first soldiers sent home on leave from Vietnam on Sunday 1st May 1966. The headline says, 'Vietnam Men "Not Talking"'.[34] There's a photo of a smiling soldier hugging a child. I'm struck by the child's expression.

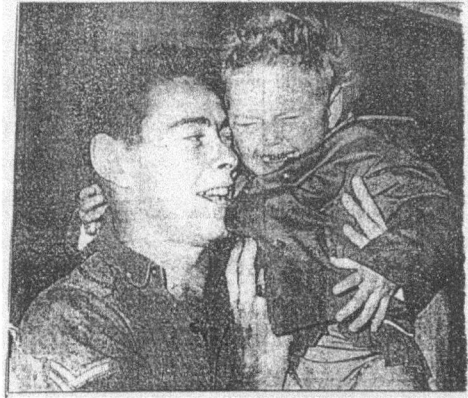

Under the photo it says:

Forty-one Australian Servicemen who returned from Vietnam yesterday were under strict orders not to say anything controversial.

There's another clipping from that time, with another child being hugged and kissed. This one looks, stony-faced, down the barrel of the lens, as if he's not really sure what is happening or who this is ... (but maybe I'm projecting).

A WELCOME HOME from his three-year-old son Robert at Mascot airport yesterday for Sergeant Dennis Saville, who won a Military Medal in Vietnam. Sergeant Saville successfully led his 25-man platoon in three hours of bitter fighting against the Viet Cong. The platoon killed three of the enemy.

Third visit to the War Memorial

I return to the War Memorial early the next day to wander through the exhibitions. On the way in from the car park, I pass gardeners bearing leaf blowers, tidying up the grounds before the crowds arrive. The autumn leaves they kick up are hit by the morning sun, and the gardeners appear, momentarily, to be floating on loud orange clouds.

I head straight for the Vietnam display in the *Conflicts 1945 to Today* section of the Memorial. One room features a helicopter full of dummies dressed in army fatigues, bearing guns. This particular display is sponsored by the noted aviator and electronics salesman Dick Smith. As I'm looking at the exhibition, a voiceover warns me that the AV display will commence soon and the room will darken. It does and, as promised, loud helicopter noises begin (though the helicopter remains static), spotlights flit around the room, over the fake grass on the floor, over the dummies, over me. Instructions shout from the speaker system and there is the sound of machine guns. Footage screening behind the helicopter shows maps, and choppers landing in the actual conflict. It is strange mix of commotion and stillness. I am still. The helicopter is still. The dummies are still. The walls are still. All else is chaos. I am in the room by myself while this is happening, until some school kids nearby hear the commotion and come to see what is happening. Once the display is over, the room falls silent again, the kids leave, and I go on with my reading, as if nothing had just happened.

There is a display panel titled *Agent Orange* about Australia's use of defoliants in Vietnam 'to destroy the jungle which sheltered the Viet Cong'. It has a paragraph about the evidence of possible health effects of exposure to the chemicals and mentions the Evatt Royal Commission in 1985 that found there was no link between exposure and some cancers or other diseases, 'though subsequent studies have allowed veterans to successfully pursue claims'. Evatt triumphantly declared the Royal Commission findings: 'Agent Orange: Not Guilty'. Later, when the findings were discredited, it emerged the Commission had 'lifted large chunks of its conclusions from the submission by Monsanto, a leading US manufacturer of defoliants'.[35]

The panel concludes, 'The War Memorial has commissioned an independent history of the medical legacies of the Vietnam War, which is expected to be completed late 2019'. The Memorial's website later said the book is due out in 2020.

I remember reading journalist Christopher Hitchens' essay about travelling to Vietnam and witnessing the devastating legacy left behind after the war. There's one line that has stayed with me – haunted me – since I read it:

> The full inventory of this historic atrocity is still being compiled … some of the victims of Agent Orange haven't even been born yet, and if that reflection doesn't shake you, then my words have been feeble and not even the photographs will do.[36]

If one of the bodies was his

There's a display panel in the War Memorial showing a photo of soldiers boarding a Qantas plane bound for Vietnam. It's the plane my dad would have been on – I think. I stand in front of it and search the shapes, trying to see if one of them could be him. It feels so futile. What difference would it make if I decided one of the bodies was his?

Considering how many people are killed, how many bodies are disfigured or maimed, how many body parts are patched together and repatriated, it's strange how little we see of the damage done to Allied bodies. Even in the War Memorial, those losses are tidied up, written as names on a plaque or symbolised by stars. All the equipment, the uniforms, soundtracks and replicas, and the reddest thing in the whole place is the poppies.

It's my last day here, so on the way out I take a detour past the diorama of Lone Pine where, in front of pastel-coloured skies, mini soldiers perpetually wage a battle against an unseen enemy (who in theory would be where I am standing). Almost 200 Australian soldiers were killed in the Battle of Lone Pine in Turkey in 1915.

I stand looking at the carefully placed figures, the immaculate detail. The central figure of a soldier is around 30cm tall. His arm is flung back, and his back is arched as though he's just been hit by a tiny bullet. Their little bodies are amazing in detail and execution but too beautiful – like artful, awful toys. The space between the soldier being shot in Turkey and me in the War Memorial looking at a model of him feels impenetrable and profound.

It is time to leave.

Birdness

Yesterday, I thought the last of the baby birds had taken flight, so I took a memorial photo of the empty nest. That afternoon though, I noticed persistent and hoarse bird calls outside the window and saw the last baby bird perched, somewhat desperately, on a branch overhanging the street. It had gone so far out on a limb that it couldn't get back.

Over the next few days, it sat in the same place, screeching, regularly and relentlessly, while the mother bird hovered nearby. She looked so small and tired, watching over her big hungry baby, willing it to fly, when she wasn't flying around herself, looking for worms.

One particularly wild and windy night, I woke a few times, worried about the baby, but it was still there in the morning, teetering forward and back and scrambling among branches to regain its balance when it tipped too far. The first two baby birds had grown fast and sure. They'd been gone a week now. This last baby hadn't fully grasped its own birdness yet.

I watched it wobbling, processing its identity. I didn't want to miss its maiden flight and was debating whether I had enough time to go and make tea when, just like that, it lost its balance completely and was forced to fly. It didn't get very far, ending up wedged between the wheelie bins and the front gate of the house across the street. The gate was shut, so once it righted itself, it could only get out by flying. The mother bird was nearby, sitting on a tree, keeping watch.

I wasn't sure whether to leave nature to its course or intervene. I saw a guy walking past, so I opened the doors and yelled at him, 'Hey, that bird's stuck. It just tried to fly for the first time.'

He looked up at me, and then at the bird behind the fence. He was a skinny young guy in a tracksuit, obviously on his way somewhere. He looked intrigued but not invested (not as much as me anyway), so I didn't think he'd hang around long. I got some clothes on and ran down. He was still there.

'That bird just tried to fly for the first time. It's stuck. What should we do? Ha. I said *we*. I've got you involved. I've been watching them for weeks, from up there.' I pointed to Adam's bedroom.

'You must be Bron.'

'What?'

I'm Brett.' We shook hands. Brett was Adam's neighbour.

'How strange. How nice to meet you. What should we do? Let's just open the gate so it can walk out. Do you think we should do anything else?'

'No,' he said smiling at me, 'I think we should just let it do its bird thing.'

And so, we did. Though I did go back inside, hover around, make a cup of tea, went upstairs to keep watch, then googled 'What to do if a baby bird falls from a nest'.

According to the *National Geographic* article I found, if it's a nestling (ugly), it's OK to pick it up and put it back in the nest, if you can find it. If it's a fledgling (cute), you should just put it out of harm's way then leave it. The article quotes Charles Eldermire, who runs the Cornell Lab of Ornithology website, where you can watch live videos of baby birds on Bird Cams. He had to put up warnings that viewers had to click on before watching the birds in the wild.

> We're aware that many have never had an unfiltered view of what happens in nature … We can learn by letting it play out. Any intervention could have a negative impact … The struggles that we go through as people in our own lives aren't all that different from the animals on the screen. The truth is, we can't control everything in our lives. One thing we can all learn from watching wild things and how they survive is that sense of resilience that is really at the core of any wild thing. [37]

Later, I went back to check on the baby bird, but it was gone.

Notes

1   'Plot Summary: *Prisoner – Cell Block H* (TV series) Episode #1.81 (1980),'
     IMDB, accessed 17 September 2019, https://www.imdb.com/title/
     tt0679152/plotsummary/.
2   John Nichols, 'Remembering the Folly of "Blank-Check" War and
     "Escalation Unlimited",' *The Nation*, 7 August 2014, https://www.thenation.
     com/article/archive/remembering-folly-blank-check-war-and-escalation
     -unlimited/.
3   Angela Phippen, 'Marsfield', *Dictionary of Sydney*, 2008,
     http://dictionaryofsydney.org/entry/marsfield.
4   Jim Robbins, *The Wonder of Birds: What They Tell Us About Ourselves,
     the World, and a Better Future* (Melbourne: Black Inc., 2017), p. 145.
5   'Roll with Units', Australian Vietnam Veterans Mortality Listing, last
     updated 9 October 2020, http://www.amvif.info/.
6   'AWM95 1/3/1 – 1–31 December 1965, Narrative, Duty Officer's log,
     Annexes', Australian War Memorial, accession number RCDIG1029191,
     https://www.awm.gov.au/collection/C1374278/.
7   'Molly's Death – *A Country Practice*', TV-Movie Bits, uploaded 18
     September 2015, https://www.youtube.com/watch?v=A88jR8oKETg.
8   'Support for children of Vietnam Veterans', Department of Veterans'
     Affairs, accessed 18 September 2020, https://www.dva.gov.au/financial-
     support/support-families/support-children-vietnam-veterans
9   Commonwealth of Australia: Foreign Affairs, Defence and Trade
     References Committee, *The Constant Battle: Suicide by Veterans*
     (Canberra: Commonwealth of Australia, 2017) , tabled 15 August 2017,
     https://www.aph.gov.au/Parliamentary_Business/Committees/Senate/
     Foreign_Affairs_Defence_and_Trade/VeteranSuicide/Report.
10   *The Constant Battle: Suicide by Veterans*, b05.
11   *The Constant Battle: Suicide by Veterans*, Submission 176, https://www.
     aph.gov.au/Parliamentary_Business/Committees/Senate/Foreign_Affairs_
     Defence_and_Trade/VeteranSuicide/Submissions.
12   *The Constant Battle: Suicide by Veterans*, Submission 317.
     (reproduced with permission)
13   *The Constant Battle: Suicide by Veterans*, Submission 317.1.
     (reproduced with permission)

14   Productivity Commission, *A Better Way to Support Veterans, Overview and Recommendations, Report no. 93*, (Canberra: Commonwealth of Australia, 2019) pp xii–vx, https://www.pc.gov.au/inquiries/completed/veterans/report/veterans-overview.pdf.

15   Gisela Kaplan, *Bird Bonds: Sex, mate-choice and cognition in Australian native birds* (Sydney: Pan Macmillan, 2019), p. 72.

16   'Taglines – *Children of a Lesser God* (1986)', IMDB, accessed 14 May 2020, https://www.imdb.com/title/tt0090830/taglines?ref_=tt_stry_tg.

17   'The Australian Origin of a Minute's Silence', Sir John Monash Centre Australian National Memorial France, posted on 8 November 2017, https://sjmc.gov.au/the-australian-origins-of-a-minutes-silence/.

18   'The Australian Origin of a Minute's Silence', Sir John Monash Centre Australian National Memorial France.

19   Heather Fishel, 'The origins and history of the Last Post', War History Online, published 8 December 2015, https://www.warhistoryonline.com/history/origins -history-last-post.html.

20   Dr Claire Weekes, *Peace from Nervous Suffering* (Sydney: Angus & Robertson – ARKON edition, 1978), p.21.

21   Personal documents released under FOI.

22   'Judgements – McGlynn, Joyce Margaret v Repatriation Commission [1981] FCA 242', Federal Court of Australia, https://www.judgments.fedcourt.gov.au/judgments/Judgments/fca/single/1981/1981FCA0242.pdf.

23   Bobbie Ann Mason, *In Country: A Novel* (New York: Harper & Row, 1985), p 36.

24   Dr Claire Weekes, *Peace from Nervous Suffering* (Sydney: Angus & Robertson, 1978), p. 132.

25   Gisela Kaplan, *Tawny Frogmouth* (Clayton South VIC: CSIRO Publishing, 2018), pp. 122–125.

26   Kathie Russo, 'Winged Migration', *This American Life 369: Poultry Slam 2008 Act Two*, https://www.thisamericanlife.org/369/poultry-slam-2008/act-two.

27   Corey Adwar, 'Inside The Vietnamese Government's Haunting War Museum – That Portrays America As The Enemy', *Business Insider Australia*, 26 August 2014, https://www.businessinsider.com.au/vietnam-war-remnants-museum-portrays-us-as-enemy-2014-8.

28   Bobbie Ann Mason, *In Country*, 226.

29   Paddy Gourley, 'Public Sector Informant: War memorial volunteers should be free to speak their minds', *Honest History*, last updated 1 September 2020, http://honesthistory.net.au/wp/wp-content/uploads/Paddy-G-1-Sept.pdf.

30   'Roll of Honour', Australian War Memorial, https://www.awm.gov.au/commemoration/honour-rolls/roll-of-honour.

31   'Brief account given my Mrs Sylvia Bink relating to the death of her son in South Vietnam', Australian War Memorial, PR 88/217 L/Cpl M Bink 9RAR Viet AWM 419/1/23.

32   'Letters from Sgt Billy Hacking to fiance, showing personal thoughts of a soldier caught up in the early phase of Australia's commitment to South Vietnam', Australian War Memorial, accession number PR00665.

33   From the scrapbook maintained by Mrs Arnison detailing the activities of 1 RAR in South Vietnam, 1965–66. Australian War Memorial Collection, Private Record PR89/006.

34   Australian War Memorial, accession number PR89/006.

35   Paul Ham, *Vietnam – The Australian War* (Sydney: Harper Collins, 2008), p. 625.

36   Christopher Hitchens, 'The Vietnam Syndrome', *Vanity Fair*, 26 March 2007, https://www.vanityfair.com/news/2006/08/hitchens200608.

37   Erika Engelhaupt, 'Should You Put a Baby Bird Back in the Nest? Depends If It's Cute', *National Geographic*, 29 June 2015, https://www.nationalgeographic.com/science/phenomena/2015/06/29/should-you-put-a-baby-bird-back-in-the-nest-depends-if-its-cute/.

List of illustrations

p. 125   Screenshot of 'Proud Son Of A Vietnam Veteran!' sticker

p. 137   A *What the Fuck* look, 2019, Bronwyn Rennex

p. 141   Dorothy W. Baruch, *You, Your Children, and War* (New York: D. Appleton-Century Company, 1943) opp. 96.

p. 159   Photo of my dad in army uniform, photographer and date unknown

p. 171   Nancy Kwan and William Holden in the 1960 film *The World of Suzie Wong*, Paramount Pictures. Reproduced under the Creative Commons Attribution-Share Alike 3.0 Unported license. https://commons.wikimedia.org/wiki/File:Nancy_Kwan_and_William_Holden_in_The_World_of_Suzie_Wong.jpg

p. 174   Photo of my dad, photographer and date unknown

p. 178   Vietnam, circa 1965, photographer unknown

p. 184   News clipping from the scrapbook maintained by Mrs Arnison detailing the activities of 1 RAR in South Vietnam, 1965–66. Australian War Memorial Collection, Private Record PR89/006, photographer unknown

p. 185   Newsclipping from the scrapbook maintained by Mrs Arnison detailing the activities of 1 RAR in South Vietnam, 1965–66. Australian War Memorial Collection, Private Record PR89/006, photographer unknown

p. 188   Darrell Ford, Richmond RAAF Base, NSW, May 1965. Troops of the 1st Battalion, The Royal Australian Regiment, Australian War Memorial Collection, FOR/65/0134/EC

p. 190–91   Lone Pine Diorama at the Australian War Memorial, Bjorn Svensson/Alamy Stock Photo

p. 192   Empty Nest, 2019, Bronwyn Rennex

p. 195   Sky, 2019, Bronwyn Rennex

Acknowledgements

Without the generous guidance and support of Dr Beth Yahp, who was my supervisor at the University of Sydney, this work wouldn't have happened. I am enormously thankful for her sensitive stewardship, a mix of kind encouragement (when I needed it most) and high expectation (when she saw the 'more' in me that I couldn't). I feel very lucky to have had her by my side while I navigated and made sense of this project.

This work also wouldn't have been possible without the generosity of my sisters, Maree and Denise. They gave me free rein to write about our family. The stories and laughs we shared as we pondered our family's silences and secrets brought us closer. Their unerring love and support made (and makes) an enormous difference to me.

Huge thanks and love to my partner Adam Dickes, for just about everything; for allowing me to include him in the work, for sharing random bird facts, for reading numerous drafts and providing kind and detailed feedback, for cooking and listening and encouraging on repeat. Thank you doesn't seem to encompass it.

For reading and providing feedback or assistance on various early drafts, I'd like to thank Janet Austin, Bethan Donnelly, Kathy Freedman, Aline Jacques, Sue Jackson, Anny Mokotow and my daughter Stella Rennex.

I've been lucky enough to have had the support, help and/or encouragement of many people along the way. Huge thanks to Christina Alvarez, Janet Austin, Liz Boyle, Stephen Boyle, Bethan Donnelly, Katy Fitzgerald, Cath Fogarty, Kathy Freedman, Suzanne Gibson, Catherine Gleeson, Jan Hutchinson, Sue Jackson, Aline Jacques, Malcolm Knox, Kate Lilley, Jane Manning, Deb Mansfield, Paul Mason, David McClymont, Anny Mokotow, Leon Morris, Tony Mott, Michelle Munro, Elena O'Keefe, Stella Rennex, Libby Sharpe, Kath Shelper and Liz Watts.

Finally, thanks to Terri-ann White for your patience and passion, and for enthusiastically taking a punt on an odd book by a late bloomer without much of a social media profile. With Upswell you are helping to foster a more diverse and interesting literary ecosystem. Long may you continue.

About Upswell

Upswell Publishing was established in 2021 by Terri-ann White as a not-for-profit press. A perceived gap in the market for distinctive literary works in fiction, poetry and narrative non-fiction was the motivation. In her years as a bookseller, writer and then publisher, Terri-ann has maintained a watch on literary books and the way they insinuate themselves into a cultural space and are then located within our literary and cultural inheritance. She is interested in making books to last: books with the potential to still be noticed, and noted, after decades and thus be ripe to influence new literary histories.

About this typeface

Book designer Becky Chilcott chose
Foundry Origin not only as a strong,
carefully considered, and dependable
typeface, but also to honour her late
friend and mentor, type designer Freda
Sack, who oversaw the project. Designed
by Freda's long-standing colleague,
Stuart de Rozario, much like Upswell
Publishing, Foundry Origin was created
out of the desire to say something new.